Sermon
Struggles

Sermon Struggles

Four Methods of Sermon Preparation

ERNEST EDWARD HUNT, III

The Seabury Press / New York

1982
The Seabury Press
815 Second Avenue
New York, N.Y. 10017

Library of Congress Cataloging in Publication Data

Hunt, Ernest Edward.
Sermon struggles.

Bibliography: p. 131
1. Preaching.   2. Sermons, American.   3. Episcopal
Church—Sermons.   I. Title.
BV4211.2.H86   251'.01   81-18344
ISBN 0-8164-2375-X   AACR2

To Elsie, who always said I could do it.

Acknowledgments

I am indebted to certain people for this work, namely the five lay persons who took the time to listen to the first eight sermons and to share their impressions with me. Those five were Dr. Nathan Marsh Pusey, vestrymember; Mr. Walter Birge, warden; Mrs. Susan Birge, chairman of the Adult Education Committee; Mrs. Janet Nelson, vestrymember, and The Rev. Jimmye Kimmey, who at the time was a lay person.

Dr. Randall Nichols, Director of the Doctor of Ministry program at Princeton Theological Seminary, challenged me time and time again to "re-write," as well as Dr. Hugh Koops of New Brunswick Seminary. Dr. Seward Hiltner previously went further and challenged me, quite properly, to be more analytical. I thank especially John Ratti of Seabury Press for his faith in the nature of this work.

Ernest E. Hunt, III

Contents

Introduction

The Problem of Preaching

There are many problems in ministry for an Episcopal clergyman and rector of a parish in New York City, but the problem that has been the most challenging to me is the regular practice of creating, researching, writing, and delivering sermons. I am sure that I am not alone in my own or any other denomination, but two reasons appear to make my personal struggle in preparing sermons more difficult than some. The first concerns the worship tradition of the Episcopal Church; as part of the Anglican Communion, it is, by and large, a liturgically-centered community of Christians. The second is my personal inclination to be a "one-method" preacher, a captive of habits of preparation accrued in the more than twenty years since my ordination.

When I state that my church is a liturgically-based communion I am not trying to construct an excuse for not preaching effectively. Yet the fact remains that the primary focus in our worship is usually the service itself, not the sermon, and that service can be the Holy Eucharist, Morning Prayer or Evening Prayer, or even the Burial Office in which eulogies, to the great relief of many, do not have a part. How many times have I heard how beautiful the Burial Service in The Book of Common Prayer is, how short, and how meaningful the prayers or music, and all without recourse to a sermon or even a short "homily," as most Roman Catholic sermons are now called.[1]

In the late 1970s Episcopalians were embroiled in a heated internal conflict over the revision of The Book of Common Prayer, but we rarely fight over reform of a preacher's way of "sermonizing" or ask for a renewal of a commitment to effective preaching. Why is the sermon secondary in position in our church, whereas in the Presbyterian, Methodist, and Congregational churches, to cite a few, the sermon is the center of attention of both the liturgy and congregation? Perhaps one answer is our historical development as a church. We are not a communion begun by a strong personality, a reformer, or an evangelist, a man like Martin Luther, John Calvin, or John Wesley. One can read much about the diplomatic skill of Archbishop Thomas Cranmer in dealing with a strong-minded English monarch or about his ability to instigate religious reforms in the country through introducing The Book of Common Prayer (the first unified service book in the vernacular) to the people of England. Yet little, if anything, is written of Cranmer's ability to preach, or of his theology. Of course, this was not true in the case of John Donne when he was dean of St. Paul's Cathedral in London, more than half a century later, or for Phillips Brooks at Trinity Church in Boston, Massachusetts, in the latter part of the 19th century; these men were great preachers but they were not beginners of churches or classical reformers. The Anglican Communion has relied on a Prayer Book since the Reformation as an anchor of worship and doctrine but it has not truly relied on the gifts of those who preach the Word of God. Anglican Stephen Sykes writes in his recent book, *The Integrity of Anglicanism*, that the "liturgy of the church creates the power base for the Christian community as a whole."[2]

However, good preaching can be found in the contemporary Episcopal Church. Any major parish will have a rector who methodically prepares a sermon for Sunday morning and in all likelihood he or she has not dashed it off at the last moment on the back of a laundry list before donning vestments. At least it is safe to say this of Manhattan, where one could cite at least three of the major parishes where preaching is genuinely serious business. On the other hand, there is a tendency in many Episcopal churches to use the liturgy as a crutch, to let the words of Holy Communion or the Gospel lesson be the Word of God without some words of a very human priest, who in fear and trembling enters the pulpit prepared to proclaim that which is faithful to the Gospel but which also helps that Gospel become the Good News of the people.

Therefore part of my conflict in preaching is a result of my religious tradition—a wonderful tradition in which I rejoice, and without which I would be lost; a rich tradition which has produced great preachers, both here and abroad. But the Anglican Church has a history of extreme variation in preaching, unlike its otherwise *via media* approach in certain areas of its corporate life. On the one hand, there is Trinity Church, Boston, with its massive, remote, towering pulpit and its own history (a mini-tradition of successive articulate clergy in the pulpit in response to high parochial expectations) and on the other hand, there is an everyday Episcopal suburban mission in which the pulpit is no larger than the lectern which often stands on the opposite side of the chancel; a small pulpit where preaching may be little more than some afterthought of a social or pastoral encounter, of a newspaper article read, or of the latest book, and of the Bible—all jelled together in a rambling, sometimes impressive, sometimes boring, ego-centered discourse.

A possible cause of this variation in preaching comes from our peculiar high and low church variations within the church. In years past a low church was usually more evangelical, more concerned with preaching than with the sacramental action at the altar, and was probably influenced by the general American evangelical tradition. On the other hand, the high church group, a sprinkling of particular dioceses and individual parishes in the Episcopal Church, grew out of the English Tractarian Movement of the 19th century, which was aimed at reform and renewal in the Church of England. When imported to America it took the dominant form of higher ceremonial usage, renewed zeal for a priestly presence, and stronger emphasis on the Eucharist. Thus, "mini-traditions" have existed within the Anglican tradition in the United States and have been kept alive in individual parishes. Even to this day, the majority of congregations which emphasize preaching will be "low churches" historically, but these groups appear to be diminishing in clearcut identity as the new (1979) Book of Common Prayer, with its combination of traditional Episcopal usage (Eucharist Rite I) and contemporary ecumenical sources (Eucharist Rite II, and its variations) takes hold of the church at large. Good preaching may no longer be identified with low church parishes per se, but with any church and with any serious occupant of the pulpit.

Another part of the Episcopal tradition which may be held responsible for the subordinate position of preaching is our special brand of seminary training. By and large, most seminaries in the Episcopal Church in America have more courses in liturgics than in homiletics. An associate of mine in my parish has had more hours in homiletics part-time in an interdenominational seminary in New York City than I had in three years in an Episcopal Seminary. I did not preach a sermon until my senior year in seminary, and that single occasion was towards the end of the last semester and in fulfillment of seminary requirements; it was preached to a small body of seminarians and two or three professors. Thumb through most of the curriculum brochures of the eleven Episcopal seminaries in the United States, and in most of them one will find liturgics emphasized more than homiletics.

But my Episcopal heritage and my seminary training were not the only reasons for my weekly struggles with sermon preparation. In some ways it was an individual, personal problem. In my parish I take the work of the Word seriously as do its lay members, and I spend hours each week on my Sunday sermon when I am slated to preach. However, I was for a long time a one-method preacher. Beginning with the lectionary for the coming Sunday, I chose a text, most likely from the Gospels—the sermon follows the reading of the Gospel—then I consulted commentaries and sat and mused awhile. If I had been reading a book about any interesting subject in any field, and that reading triggered a certain creative response in me personally, then I often chose to incorporate themes from the book in my sermon. Usually I was inclined to write in one long, brainstorming session; and once all my free-flowing thoughts were on paper, handwritten (if it was 3:00 A.M.) or typed, I organized my thoughts and examples through repeated drafts which could take from ten to fifteen hours of time in the course of the week. Someone has said that the clergy should spend one hour in preparation for each minute the sermon takes to preach—and I have. Yet I had not learned to vary methods of preparation, and did not reflect on what really prompted my long hours in writing a sermon. The fact is that preaching is an important aspect of parish ministry, and it is plain hard work which takes time away from being a pastor. A modern clergyman plays many roles: administrator, counselor, teacher, worship leader, community leader, and preacher; but among all the roles given a pastor today, one of the most demanding is that of being an effective preacher and communicator.

Because I did consider preaching a vital part of my total ministry and a part that was difficult for me, I began to consider carefully what constituted an effective sermon and whether or not the preparation method I used had a special impact on the power of the sermon and its ultimate impact on the people who heard it. Because I am aware that I am not alone among clergy and laity in my sermon struggles, it seemed useful to put my thoughts down in this book for others to use in analyzing and improving the effectiveness of their own sermons.

I have limited my investigation to two vital aspects of the sermon process, the preparation of the sermon and the hearing response to it. I have not changed the texts of the sermons used to illustrate this discussion. They are as they were when first preached.

The most important factor to me in the writing of any sermon is not so much its ultimate style or presentation, but the struggle I went through in writing it. Therefore, I pose the question, does the struggle (the conflict and the creativity) experienced by the preacher in his office or his study have anything to do with the eventfulness of preaching as a communicative fact? Does the way one works at producing a sermon influence the response? For too long I placed myself in a "box," so to speak, typecast by not being free enough, or confident enough, to experiment with different approaches to a sermon. The temptation in sermon preparation has been to make of it another chore, a routine job, instead of a creative and varied process.

In order to determine whether varying and perhaps interesting methods of preparation have any real effect on a congregation, I have kept track of my conflict in preparation, while keeping my sermon presentation the same. And I have compared my diary or weekly "history" of my sermon struggles with the recorded reactions of a listening group to the sermon. I preached eight sermons with different methods of preparation and selected five committed laypersons to be a hearing response group which would meet and record its reactions to the sermon each time I preached. I also include four other sermons which illustrate the methods of sermon preparation I use.

At the beginning of my study I realized that it had been years since I had thought much about how I prepared a sermon. Therefore, I decided to vary processes of preparation, to provide a record of the data of a selected method, and to compare the results of that method to the comments of my response group. This approach is quite different from my usual way of doing things.

I am by nature probably very much like my Welsh grandmother who lived with our family until she died at the age of 86. She would prepare what we called "bake stones," a type of soft flat biscuit with raisins, but she would never tell us what ingredients she used or provide us a recipe. Therefore we were not only dependent on her for an exotic treat—we couldn't replicate her culinary art. We never did discover whether she purposefully chose to keep her Welsh cakes a secret or if she really didn't know how to tell us exactly what to do; perhaps it was just second nature to her. If the latter was the case, then it would mean that bake stones were an "intuitive" matter with her and that she had never learned to reflect on what she did in order to share it with others. Because she was almost totally deaf since birth, and one of fourteen children, she may not have known how to communicate something she had learned somewhere as a child, or perhaps she may have been a little paranoid!

I came to realize that I had been writing sermons much as my grandmother made Welsh cakes. What I hope is that this book will make the reader more conscious of a written "recipe," and more willing to try different recipes, not so much to see how the cake looks but what different recipes do to the taste. Does changing a recipe enhance the cake, or does it have little effect on its taste? Does varying the method of a sermon produce a better response?

Although I am aware of the variables, ranging from how a preacher feels on a given Sunday to how some listeners in the congregation feel about the preacher, I still believe that the investigation of purposefully varied methodologies can reveal whether or not the creative conflict to produce a sermon has a direct effect on the response of those who listen to it. Therefore my purpose has been to analyze the dynamics of sermon preparation with reference to its outcome. Does struggle, whether in me personally or with a particular method, relate to a heightened experience of the listening group?

This book is designed to help the preacher avoid or get over the "Johnny-one-note" approach to sermon preparation, to free the preacher to experiment with different approaches or methods with which to reach his or her congregation most effectively. It seems important that one understand the precise definition of the word *method* as it will be used in this discussion. *Method* is the process of beginning, researching, writing, and concluding a sermon *before* it is preached. Although I am not a systematic thinker by nature, I have learned to be systematic when necessary. I have chosen four methods for sermon preparation (to be discussed in detail later): the *text method*, the *cultural source method*, the *pastoral situation method*, and the *conflict method*.

Each method is based on some theological assumptions. The

text method emphasizes primary Biblical sources and a theology of transcendence. The *cultural source method* uses the inspiration of literature or the daily newspaper and relies more on a theology of immanence. The *pastoral situation method* is concerned with the problems of individuals and society and is based on a "transformation of society" motif, or an outreach of mercy and compassion for all. The *conflict method* is based on a theology of tension, a dialectic between the text and an argument with or against it, and a search for a synthesis of meaning between Biblical source and everyday reality. The first chapter explains in detail the basis for my underlying theological assumptions, as well as my reasons for identifying a theological emphasis for each method.

NOTES

1. *The New York Times* referred to a spontaneous sermon by Pope Paul VI in Poland as a "homily" on its front page on June 3, 1979.

2. Stephen Sykes, *The Integrity of Anglicanism,* p. 103.

1

Theological Basis of Preaching

It is important for one who is responsible for presenting the Word of God to share with his readers a theology which undergirds a personal struggle to be creative in his sermon preparation. Preaching reflects the developed viewpoint of the preacher. Preaching can move persons to self-reflection, deeper commitment, and a broader understanding of the church and of leading Christian thinkers of the past and present.

Preaching is an experience of the cross; the struggle to live with and for others is involved in an effort to prepare a sermon which genuinely "touches" people and reveals something of God's working in me, my past, my encounters with people, and my judgments and decisions. Thus preaching can assist others to discern the living God working in their lives; he is a God who leaves no one alone (not even the preacher). He is an active, almost interfering, yet always supporting God in our developing, evolving passage from birth to death, in our passage from the earliest Christian awakening of the soul to a more mature sense of sanctification.

My own theology developed through three "passages." The first was my conversion to Christianity and the Episcopal Church while at Stanford University; the second was my study in the Episcopal Theological Seminary of the Southwest in Austin, Texas; and the third has been my continued theological development since ordination in 1959, the longest passage of all.

I turned to Christianity from agnosticism, and a California background bereft of church experience, through two main sources: elective courses in religion at Stanford University and an introduction to the Episcopal Church through friends.

As a college freshman, I was like a newborn baby who drank deeply from the milk of knowledge which was presented to me by my most interesting course, "Western Civilization." This was a year's overview of history from Mesopotamia to World War II, and included sociology, anthropology, philosophy, and religion. I became a history major, and since I argued against the need for institutional religion and for certain relatively atheistic views represented by Sartre or Camus, I decided to reinforce my position that ethical behavior did not need deity by taking a comparative religion course. I learned about Tibetan ghost traps and Japanese Shinto shrines; I admired the Buddha for leaping over his palace wall and leaving behind riches for the sake of finding inner peace. My interest in religion grew. I took an Old Testament course from a jovial rabbi who compared Genesis with the Gilgamesh epic, and who claimed the basic tension in the Old Testament was between the nomadic Hebrew Father-God and the Canaanite's female fertility religion. A Presbyterian named Alexander Miller then taught me New Testament, and not only did I read his *Renewal of Man* twice but I remember his discussion class on St. Paul's words:

> I do not do the thing I want, but I do the very thing I hate. . . . Who will deliver me from this body of death?

These words touched me deeply. They helped me to realize that my conflicts about ethics, and about the paradox between good and evil, were also conflicts experienced by a saint and apostle of the church. With Paul's personal conflict goading my own religious awakening, I attended church services with friends. I recall quite clearly one Sunday an Episcopal priest pronouncing absolution, or declaration of God's forgiveness, and I was inwardly moved. I think it was then that I decided to be a Christian and to become baptized and confirmed. Later, reading some of the literature in vogue at the time which was written by Anglicans T. S. Eliot and W. H. Auden, I studied the Episcopal Church and determined, after family conflicts, to pursue a vocation as an ordained clergyman.

My second "passage" was stimulated by my special interests in seminary and by the theological focus of the Episcopal Seminary of the Southwest in the years I was there (1956–59). The seminary offered classical reformed theology and a wide curriculum of courses in mission theology and in theology and literature. I was influenced by the works of Barth, Bonhoeffer, and Brunner, mainly because Paul Van Buren (author of *Christ in Our Place* and *The Secular Meaning of the Gospel*) taught them in dogmatic theology. I became a neo-Barthian and was only superficially exposed to the works of Paul Tillich; so one might say that I was an S.O.B., a son of Barth who in turn appreciated Bonhoeffer and especially the works of Reinhold Niebuhr and H. Richard Niebuhr. On the other hand, William Clebsch (author of *Pastoral Care in Historical Perspective, England's Earliest Protestants,* and *American Religious Thought*) introduced me to a broader spectrum which included the thought of Hegel, of Schleiermacher, and encompassed the idea of the need for natural revelation. Since Clebsch taught history and missions, I became aware then that congregational religious expression was indigenous to America, and through Clebsch's influence I immersed myself in the Kramer/Hocking debate concerning the nature of world missions. At the same time another professor, who taught Christian themes in world literature, helped me to discover the anguished faith of Dostoevski and the religious struggle of Herman Melville.

In terms of Anglican thought, I paid little attention to Elizabethan theologian Richard Hooker, but spent hours reading the poetry, meditations, and sermons of John Donne. It is said that Donne was the first existentialist because of his analytical approach to poetry. His personal conflicts as well as his use of the imagery of dialectical theology impressed me. I also spent three months in a rural village of Mexico through the auspices of the now defunct Overseas Mission Training Program, and I began to consider all ministry as missionary, whether in the United States or abroad.

I was graduated from seminary with honors, but after a week of canonical examinations in the diocese of California I was told by an examiner that I was deficient in New Testament. Consequently, I was prohibited from preaching for six months (and as a deacon I could not celebrate the Eucharist either) yet I was given a rural mission to rebuild, a new mission to build, and Soledad Correctional Facility in which to organize a part-time chaplaincy. The late Bishop James Pike, who disagreed with the examining chaplains and later dismissed them, revoked their decision about me and I was allowed to preach fairly soon after ordination. But I suppose I have been making up for that early censure ever since.

After ordination, I began my third passage. I continued to read and expand my own theological thought by earning an M.A. in Hispanic-American studies and religion at Stanford University, by attending several sessions of the College of Preachers in Washington, D.C., and by entering the D. Min. program at Princeton Theological Seminary. My thesis at Stanford was a painstaking search for native Protestant theologies of Latin America. I discovered only eight indigenous thinkers, but my understanding that different cultures needed differing theologies enriched my understanding of ministry. My adjustment from a rural church to a suburban parish, and now to an urban congregation, came and comes in part from my belief that theology results from encounter with culture.

At the College of Preachers where I was a fellow in residence in 1975 I wrote a substantial paper on contemporary evangelicals and compared them to classical Anglican evangelicals. I also refined my interest in the thought of Nicolas Berdyaev, an exile from Russia who wrote volumes of philosophy and of Christian reflection before his death in 1948 in Paris. I pursued his thought for two reasons: the first, my interest in Dostoevski, and later, Solzhenitsyn; the second, my lasting impression of one Merrill Hutchins, a former Baptist missionary who decided to return to seminary in the Episcopal Church, even though he had terminal leukemia. He taught at the University of Texas while finishing a year at our seminary in 1958; and he quoted Berdyaev almost every time I heard him speak. I will never forget, for example, this quotation of Hutchins from Berdyaev: "Neither the bourgeois of the West nor the proletariat of the East, but the aristocracy of the Spirit." Hutchins died soon after he was ordained.

Added to my experiences in postgraduate work has been my experience of ministry and my continual search to preach to the issues of life—to evil and suffering, goodness and joy, to the everyday life of men and women, and to the realistic hope Christ offers us all. Moltmann's *Crucified God* was an important book, which I read for the very beginning of my doctoral work in 1975. Moltmann identified God not so much with revolution or resurrection, both real and necessary, but with the God who suffers for us and with us, through the Holocaust, through terminal illnesses, and through airplane crashes. Hope is a cross transformed from an instrument of death to a symbol of new life.

With this background I determined four main theological assumptions which formed my world view and which are at the heart of my struggle to preach.

Theological Assumptions

My first premise is that we exist in a "moral universe." There is ultimate justice, known to the ancient Greeks as the "judgments of God in time are moral" or to Christians as the belief that Christ at the end of history will win the victory of his Kingdom in righteousness. However, we are subject to coincidence, circumstance, and incompletion because of the freedom given us by God. He is not a dictator who has made all things perfect for us; if this were the case, we would be his puppets on a string always loving him. Yet our freedom leaves us vulnerable to natural calamity, social exploitation, and mistaken personal decision. We miss the mark, as the Hebrews described the nature of sin: evil is freedom used in license, it is the combination of forces which oppose righteousness and which come from within people and from the fallible institutions of society. Reinhold Niebuhr's book, *Moral Man and Immoral Society,* rightly affirms that while one may try to be ethical, morality always breaks down in community. Yet evil was also summed up in the Cross as a symbol of execution, as all deity was contained in him who died on Golgotha. His victory over evil, however, is realized only in part.

Paul Van Buren once made a comparison between D-Day and VE-Day in relation to the Cross and to the Second Coming. Imagine yourself, he would say, as a member of the Underground fighting the Nazis in Europe in 1944. One day on the radio you hear the good news that a powerful force has been launched against your enemies whom you consider to be evil and tyrannical. Even though you may suffer and perhaps die, you know there will be a VE-Day in the future and that the evil you may still have to fight will eventually be overcome. In the meantime, one can hope—even though one may be discovered and destroyed. This illustration is one way to understand that we live under the reign of Christ until his Kingdom is fully realized.

While not a "process" theologian per se, I understand and appreciate what Teilhard de Chardin meant by ultimate consummation of human life, history, and the universe, but I hesitate to exclude from my world view "another world," be it called the Kingdom of God (in its totality), life in God, the Kingdom of Heaven, the life of the Spirit, of ultimate freedom, emancipated from secular determinism (Nicholas Berdyaev), or the discovery of the ideal life, the vision of heavenly perfection (C. S. Lewis). Herman Melville's writings are important to me precisely because of this American author's struggle with ultimate justice. Too many people have suffered, have led incomplete lives, are "dead" to us for there not to be ultimate justice and a more complete life as evidenced by the resurrection of Jesus of Nazareth.

With my second assumption that there is a "life in God" which can be known only in part in this life—but is "another life in totality"—I have come to understand the Incarnation as the breakthrough of divinity into history in Jesus (our flesh) Christ (the name of the risen victory of the new man). Society can therefore be transformed or changed, except as such change is thwarted by the sinfulness in human structures and the nature of tragedy in circumstance, because there is a kingdom to which this life can be compared and which provides motivation for redemption. The Church, as the Body of Christ which reaches out to the world and to individuals as Christ's arms on the cross reach out to embrace brokenness, elevates man as a sacred individual when he would otherwise be considered a number, or a member of the masses.

Yet no person is saved in isolation from his brothers and sisters; ultimately there is social salvation in the sense of a cosmic salvation, as Nicholas Berdyaev wrote in *Freedom and the Spirit,* because Christ's coming to us, his death and resurrection, has already begun the redemptive process of history and creation. Therefore a theology of mission is sharing the Good News of what has happened to the world through Christ with man, who in ignorance or disobedience hears only the news of self, society, and the natural process. He often elevates such knowledge from secular sources to ultimate, almost idolatrous levels from his need for oneness with the ultimate Other. Such action is a sign of our sinfulness, original to each of us.

However, the Spirit of God which is at work in the world regardless of human sin and secular determinism can awaken man to the Good News through "cultural sources." For example, C. S. Lewis writes that poetry, literature, experiences with sorrow or death, can turn an individual towards a growing appreciation and love of God. Immanence can turn one to transcendence while transcendence causes us to look for God in each person.

My third assumption is that the Crucifixion/Resurrection of Jesus Christ is the key to the existential mystery of human beings—in understanding themselves, each other, and the world. This mystery pervades the pastoral and psychological dimensions of man. I can read Camus or Freud and find "absurdity," alienation, or psychopathic behavior quite in keeping with a world in tension with its fallen nature and the redemption in Christ, with a world which, in freedom, produces the terrible brokenness of the cross. Yet I can also say, as a man of faith, that there *is* an exit from the human hell of crippled and demented relationships, or of cruel and seemingly meaningless circumstance. God suffers with us and shares the tension between his Kingdom and the kingdoms of this world.

And my fourth assumption is that Holy Scripture, the teachings of the church fathers, apostolic tradition, and the early creeds (not literally in each case but as part of the sacred story of salvation) are the bedrock—must be the bedrock—of my theology. Since Scripture is the standard for my theology, I always use a text in some way when preaching. I must not only be faithful to the meaningfulness of Holy Writ in relation to the liturgy, but must also, as a preacher, more importantly, be faithful to the Biblical witness. Stephen Crites writes that the narrative quality of human experience expresses itself in three dimensions: the first, sacred story (or myth with ultimate and religious depth); the second, mundane story (or expression of values and attitudes of a natural source); the third, the temporal experience itself (expressed tensions from life). My interpretation of the sacred story is stated thus: Jesus was born to Mary and developed a growing consciousness of his destiny (as we possess a growing understanding of salvation in terms of maturation and sanctification); he chose freely (as opposed to determinism and as expression of human free will) his terror-filled call, sharing our agony of decision; he endured the cross and its shame, and God elevated his name above all names (the New Man of Resurrection); he, or the Spirit, works to elevate each individual to a sense of the sacredness of his own story, of the story of others, and of the story of life. His "temporal" experience is not dissimilar to ours. The mundane stories of his life, his people, of history, and of all human experience cross at the Cross with the Sacred Story.

Yet Christ is Lord and he is the pattern for all personhood. He is both divine and human. I am not Schleiermacherian in that I believe the divinity of Christ lies in his own consciousness of his unique relation to God; this position is too close to adoptionism or some sort of salvation through conscious psychological compatibility with deity. On the other hand, Christ's incarnation is not such a "radical breakthrough" in Jesus alone that it denies the results of incarnation *on* creation and society. Jesus reveals the mystery of incarnation through the developments of his life and decisions which led him to be seen voluntarily as the Messiah by his disciples and followers. I believe he had a growing awareness of who he was, much as we mature, on our own level, in our awareness of who we are. I am reminded of Lewis Sherrill's *The Struggle of the Soul* in which confrontation with stages in life leads to spiritual and psychological maturation, but Christ's spiritual summit was way beyond our reach. If he were not unique, divine, and different from us, then "God could not have reconciled the world unto Himself," and if he were not fully man, then we would have the docetic problem which allows us to deny matter and affirm only spirit. Union of spirit and matter are evidenced in the Incarnate One; he is our unity and our peace. God is the perfect union of judgment and love (his love is his judgment and his judgment is love). In us love and judgment are often polarized, that is, we love too much and become possessive, or we love too little and reject others. Jesus Christ is the unique Son of God who uplifts all men to be sons of God through his death and resurrection.

In regard to the church I consider it to be Catholic, Apostolic, and, by intention, One. While I accept the Reformers' notion that Scripture is the basis of doctrine, I hold that doctrine, as the limbs of a spreading, growing tree (the roots of course being Scripture) can and should change according to the needs and insights of contemporary man, the conditions of contemporary life, and the beckoning of the Spirit. All of which is in tension with the essence of Scripture, with a moral universe, and with the basic tradition of the church. Preaching is proclaiming Christ as Lord and man as possessing unique dignity because of him.

Transcendence (the life of God beyond the world), immanence (the incarnate life of God in the world or his expression of himself and his will in nature), transformation (the transfiguration of man and the mission of compassion and Good News to the world), and temporal tension (existential crucifixion and resurrection, conflict and creativity) are ways to express theological truths behind preaching.

Theological Emphases of Methods

As I began to define and develop different methods of sermon preparation, it became clear to me that certain theological motifs informed my thinking and my preaching. Because my theology is basically neo-orthodox, Holy Scripture for me is a source for the Word of God which the newspaper is not. I do not deny that God speaks to us in poetry or sources other than Scripture, but I do affirm that the Old and New Testaments contain unique revelations of God to humankind, even though "immanence," "transformation," and "tension" are also in Holy Scripture. Scripture itself cannot be so easily compartmentalized as was done in developing a theological basis for each method, but for the first time in my life I discovered what these assumptions were and how they influenced my preaching.

Obviously, revelation occurs in "cultural sources," a process which I describe later, or in any life situation, but my way has been to separate Holy Writ from poetry, prose, and the newspaper. Scripture has been tested by time and the church and contains God's word more clearly than some recent secular discovery. And although I do not deny that God speaks outside the Bible, Scripture is an anchor and the means by which we discern whether or not what is currently popular is faithful to the one revealed story. I therefore accept the reformer's rule of thumb; Scripture is the standard of revelation about God. But as an Anglican, I am happy to test this standard at any time or place with what arises from culture. To me ethics and mission are based on Christian theology and tradition, which places me more in the tradition of Barth than of Tillich.

Yet as different methods were used in sermon preparation and an effort was made to understand each theologically, I realized that method and theology overlapped. How can one have transcendence without immanence? How can one preach to a pastoral situation without conflict and tension between a given problem area and Holy Scripture? Even though I am aware that the four methods of preparation discussed here are not entities by themselves, the results of my study prove that methods and theological bases for methods overlap. I also discovered that no clear-cut differentiation existed in theology for each method. However, at the beginning of this project a theology of preaching from a text seemed to me to emphasize transcendence more than immanence because of my belief that the Word of God derived more from Scripture than from any secular source. Yet this project taught me that transcendence, immanence, transformation, and temporal conflict were not only included in all my sermons but also part of my methodological approach to sermons and integral parts of my personal theology. Therefore, read the following with an understanding that theological emphases and different methods did indeed overlap as I analyzed the results of my work later.

The Textual Method

The theology of preparing a sermon from a text is one which keeps faith with the words of those persons who witnessed in Biblical times. By staying close to the original meaning and by understanding the source, style, and life situation of a passage from Scripture, its truth may be revealed, perhaps a timeless truth applied to the present day. Yet it is not that my emphasis in this approach relegates the contemporary world to a secondary position; it is rather that the words in the Word of God possess enough truth to speak to the present, depending upon my own sensitivity and understanding of its time and place. Scripture is the standard for theology, the Reformers believed, and so the *textual method keeps faith with Scripture more than with a current piece of literature.* In summary, let me identify this method as using a theology of transcendence, more a Barthian "breakthrough" of the Word of God into the world than the Spirit of God revealed in the world. This is the theology of "sacred story."

Cultural Sources Method

The theology of beginning from a piece of literature or from the newspaper necessarily implies that God is at work in the world; we look for signs of his activity through men and women of good will. This may be more incarnational preaching, more an emphasis such as that of F. D. Maurice who taught that God was already at work in society. In this method, however, I have tried to reconcile the "otherness" of God with the immanence of God, with natural theology, with God's Spirit at work in the lives of all people. In this approach I have tried to be sensitive to his word and his will for his world, his word outside Scripture. I identify this method as one which utilizes a *theology of immanence,* and is of "mundane story."

The Pastoral Situation Method

The theology of preaching to a pastoral situation is one in which God reveals himself in the suffering and needs of all people. For example, Mother Teresa of India has stated that because of the poor, to whom she ministers, she discovers Christ—and not in spite of them. The church witnesses to God's mercy and compassion for all people. Pastoral needs are addressed because, in my opinion, the church is called to transform society, as H. R. Niebuhr advocated in his book, *Christ and Culture.* We address social wrongs; it is the challenge of the preacher to transform (not necessarily to reform or correct) society as a spokesman for the church, and he or she may at times stand in judgment on social sin, or at least bring a perspective to society which it would not have without some reference to ultimacy. Therefore, this method might be termed a *theology of transformation of the world,* where sacred story intersects mundane story.

The Conflict Method

We live in an imperfect world. I am a sinful man, and there is brokenness in life. Sometimes that brokenness wells up within me as I confront Scripture. Any tension between the real and the ideal is revealed here as well, and that tension—a theology of tension—between opposites or extremes is also revealed, perhaps as I argue with a text or share temporal experience, my anxiety about its application to the present and to the needs of people. I therefore define this method as using *a theology of tension,* and it is a method of "temporal experience."

Certain conclusions about the theology behind my preaching have been presented which derived from my conversion, my seminary experience, and my years in the ministry. The four methods contained certain theological motifs or emphases which resulted from my own perceptions. As the findings of my study emerged, I discovered that each method used included all four theological emphases—and this fact intrigued me. I now know the whole of my own theological underpinnings more clearly, and perceive that not only transcendence, immanence, transformation, and conflict are parts of each sermon I preached but are also part of my own personal theological outlook. I began this work with four areas of theology to match four distinct methods, all of which can be found in my personal history as a theologically changing and developing Christian and pastor. The whole of my own theological perceptions are much more clearly understood now because of this project. I hope the reader will come to a similar understanding of his or her own theological perceptions as a result of reading about it.

2

Procedures

This project was a deliberate construction of varied methods of preaching to be tested against the communicative response of a group of people who volunteered to listen to each sermon, discuss it after it had been preached, and provide information from their meetings as data for my consideration and evaluation. There were three major procedures involved. The first was the discipline of the preacher moving in four distinctly different ways from text or source to sermon in a set of eight sermons. The second was the preacher's effort to keep the finished product the same, that is, four pages of double-spaced typewritten words delivered in my own conventional style, and the consequent eight sermons themselves. The third was the establishment of a feedback group of five persons who were as free as possible to articulate individual experiences of the sermon. My task was to sift through the evidence from the words of the group and compare it to the way in which the Word was prepared.

After much reading and research, I chose four ways of preparing sermons. In addition to a method of preparation being defined as a process of researching, beginning, writing, and concluding a sermon before it is preached, I have, for practical purposes, also considered a method to be a conscious direction of preparation emanating from a different source each time I approached writing a sermon.

The first of the four ways was suggested by my reading *Design for Preaching* by Grady Davis and *How Shall They Hear* by G. W. Ireson, published some time ago by SPCK. In the first Davis advocates a normal propositional method in which the text is always source; in the Ireson book, a sermon moves from text through introduction, presentation, and application or conclusion. The direction in this propositional method, or what I would prefer to call "text method," flows from text, through analysis of meaning by commentary. Next, the preacher's imagination (his own creativity in relation to his fidelity to the Scriptures and to the Faith) is engaged, which in turn are united to his own experience (his own "personal history" as Bultmann once stated) through cultural sources (I mean literature, artful quotations, newspaper articles, sociological statements, psychology) to the pastoral situation, or "where it hurts in the pew."

The second method is one which is suggested by Robert Raines in *Creative Brooding,* although the book is not actually about preaching. In his book, Raines appears to use a newspaper article or a piece of writing by a well-known author, then moves with Biblical faithfulness but with little conceptualization to a text and a pastoral situation. While he is true to the Biblical "mind" his way is not classic by any means, but proceeds from "cultural sources" through imagination, to text, to pastoral situation.

The third way was one suggested by the famous preacher Harry Emerson Fosdick. In this way, preparation has to do with envisioning a recipient of the sermon, a hypothetical person whose problem is in some way addressed by the underlying text. In other words, Fosdick would begin with the pastoral situation. Clyde Fant in *Preaching for Today* quotes Fosdick as saying: "Start with a life issue, a real personal or social problem, face that problem squarely, deal with it honestly, and throw such life on it from the spirit of Christ, that people will be able to think more clearly and live more nobly because of that sermon."[1] Therefore the direction in this method is from "pastoral situation" through imagination to text, with possible use of cultural sources to follow.

The final method was suggested by Randall Nichols in his doctoral dissertation at Princeton Theological Seminary. I personally call Nichols' approach the conflict method. He writes:

> What both the conflict in creativity point of view and crisis in theology point of view share is the principle that reality is dialectical, critical, conflictual.[2]

My own understanding of a "conflict" methodology is informed by the dialectical method—thesis, antithesis, synthesis—or the back-and-forth dialogue in the "straw man" method. Sometimes I am antagonized by a text or personally and spiritually upset by it, and my own negative response to it can produce a creative sermon. Other times I have used a Kafka or Camus text as rebuttal, for example, to a text from Scripture, or to some of the unsolved theological problems as they affect each individual life. My own love/hate relationship with Scripture, or with some of the "brokenness of life" can produce a sermon. Therefore this method could be considered an inversion of number one, or its shadow. Let me propose that one does begin with a text, but reacts against it personally, then analyzes its meaning, disagrees, and supports one's own negative feelings with cultural sources in order to speak to a pastoral situation. While I am indebted to Randall Nichols for stimulating my thinking in a dialectical manner in this method, I think I have formed my own way of conceiving a "conflict" method.

Record from Source to Sermon
On each occasion of sermon preparation I have kept notes to record how I was seized by certain ideas or situations, followed by a statement of the intention of the sermon. I have also kept a record of the struggle and sources for each method, as well as marking the time taken for writing each sermon. I have included in my documentation any eccentricities and outside influences which helped or thwarted my initial purpose. After

consciously following a certain method, I have kept a record of all my sources, such as current events or hymns. For example, a favorite hymn which meant much to me partially inspired one method I used. An outline of my record in general was as follows:

- Sources of inspiration
- Choice of method
- Statement of intention of the sermon
- Progress and conflict
- Documentation of sources
- Number of drafts and time taken
- Last minute changes of thought
- Final result and possible revised statement of intention

Sermons Preached
I preached the eight sermons that appear here in my parish church in New York City in a six-month period. The context of each sermon will be partially discussed in relation to my notes and to the reactions of the sermon feedback group. Each sermon was in completed form as similar to another as possible; I did not purposely change my style of presentation and I used my four-page manuscript which I basically read but in such a way that it was not obvious. I usually began with an opening sentence which was a clue to a main point conclusion.

The first sermon was called "Expanded Horizons, not Expanded Egos," and preached at the 11:00 A.M. service before the Annual Meeting of the parish. It was based on the second method beginning from literature, or a news article, in this case an article in the Stanford University "Observer" taken from the works of John Gardner, former Secretary of Health.

The second sermon was entitled "Loneliness," and was inspired by the loneliness of patients at the great urban hospitals near the church, particularly Memorial Sloan-Kettering Cancer Center. In this sermon I used the third method, "pastoral situation."

The third sermon was called "Participation," and was a result of the conflict method and my contention that forgiveness is less easy to realize than our guilt.

The fourth sermon was preached on the first Sunday in Lent, and again was a "conflict" sermon arising from my tension with wilderness as conceived by some to be only rural and not urban. It was entitled "The Wilderness of the City."

The fifth sermon, preached after I had returned from a visit to my father in California, was a "pastoral situation" sermon about the terminal suffering of my father. I used the third method.

The sixth sermon was inspired by my favorite hymn, "Once to Every Man and Nation," and utilized the second method, a source other than a Biblical text.

The seventh sermon was preached on Palm Sunday, was called "Now or Else," was text-based, employed method number one, and concerned the triumphal entry of Christ into Jerusalem.

The eighth and last sermon was on Easter Sunday, was titled "Empty Tombs Mean Full Lives," and was also text-based, using, again, the first method.

Each sermon ended with a conclusion which in some way restated some of the opening statement. An outline of all the sermons followed this course:

- Opening statement (the first paragraph usually).
- A flow of argument which always used the text in some way and other sources.
- A closing summary which echoed the opening.

Hearing Response Group

I originally asked six active lay members of the church to be on a committee which would listen to my sermons and then discuss in a group what they had heard. My first inclination was to meet with them and to have them question me, but again, after consulting my advisors, I realized that my presence would not leave the committee free to discuss what I had preached. I did not want to intimidate them accidentally, so I asked if someone could either tape or take minutes of their meeting and present the evidence of their "struggle" to me as soon as possible after the preaching event. They agreed. However, the layperson who had volunteered to tape the sessions was out of town for the first meeting and eventually dropped out of the experiment. I consulted the group about whether or not to replace him and about the method of recording their response. They unanimously agreed that a sixth person was not needed and that their "life together" had already begun and should continue as it was. A laywoman of profound theological sensitivity volunteered to take minutes, to double-check her written responses to those of the individual speakers, and to present them to me within a few days after the Sunday sermon. At first they questioned me as to how they should respond, and I told them to try to stay away from evaluating the sermon and to share their own experiences of the sermon and the experiences triggered in their minds and spirits *by* the sermon.

I asked Nathan M. Pusey, former president of Harvard University and vestryman of my church, to be the convenor of the group, which originally comprised Tom Tull, director of the National Institute for Lay Training of the Episcopal Church and a vestryman; Jimmye Kimmey, a woman, former professor, television interviewer, community leader, and later, seminarian and then priest; Walter Birge, headmaster of the Town School in New York City and warden of the vestry; Susan Birge, his wife and an active participant in our adult forum and a member of the adult education committee; Janet Nelson, a marathon runner, adult education committee member, and a vestry member. Mr. Tull, due to a job change, resigned, and the five others continued. I chose this group because they were highly committed members of the parish and because they could also commit themselves to attending church on the Sundays I was slated to preach.

The clerk, Jimmye Kimmey, took excellent notes, always asking probing questions and rechecking her responses. She generally discussed the results with me personally as she handed me her minutes the following week.

I asked the committee not to judge style, delivery, or my

presence; but to stay with what enabled them to articulate an experience, their feelings, and memories in relation to their own joy or suffering, their own interpretations of the meaning of life, their own sense of being caught up in the sermon and why. The question "why?" was important, so that they might speak freely about themselves, their lives, even the sort of day they had had or the worries which were on their minds. I asked them not to judge a good sermon or a bad sermon because we did not establish criteria for this purpose, but as the reader will discover later, the group, when alone, acted like most groups, being themselves, and even sometimes giving me "high marks" or expressing some disappointment.

My aim was for them to provide me with their honest impressions and reactions so that I could compare their responses to my struggle in the preparation of the sermon. I also intended to compare their responses, sermon to sermon, but I chose not to inform them of any variation of method on my part. As far as they were concerned, they were hearing a sermon based on an unknown way of preparation. It was not even mentioned as a possibility and so was not a part of their challenge from me. I asked simply for "articulated experiential response" so that I could later compare what they said about each sermon with each sermon. A summary of each group response follows my diary of writing each sermon, as well as a digest of the sermon itself. In addition, I present in the next four chapters four other sermons with accompanying diaries, thus giving the reader further examples of each preparation method.

NOTES

1. Clyde Fant, *Preaching for Today*, p. 22.

2. Randall Nichols, *Conflict and Creativity: The Dynamics of the Communicative Process in Theological Perspective*, p. 351.

3

The Text Method

In this chapter three sermons, plus personal records of the writing of each, as well as a hearing response from lay people for the first two sermons, are presented for the reader's consideration. This first of the four methods I have mentioned treats the text itself as the primary source for the inspiration of the sermon. The best way for me to proceed in this method is to read the lessons for the coming Sunday, assuming that these are available either from the lectionary of a particular denomination or, as in my case, from the every Sunday lectionary in The Book of Common Prayer. The Episcopal Church has a three-cycle system, years A,B,C, in an effort to include more variety of Holy Scripture in lessons than in the past.

The direction in this text method flows from a Scriptural passage one is most comfortable preaching from, through analysis of the passage by one's favorite commentary or commentaries, through the preacher's own imagination and creativity, through "cultural sources" (clippings from the newspaper which he or she may have saved or a book one has been reading), through the words of a hymn, to the pastoral situation, or a focus of need in the congregation, community, or world at large.

Three things usually occur to me as I read an interesting

passage, or as I am forced to deal with a certain text. The first is that the passage generally stimulates my curiosity. I need to find out more about the background of the writing, the history of the times, and the sociology of the period. Therefore good commentaries are essential, and preaching without consulting them is intellectually risky. It may be that you think you know all about Romans or the Gospel of Luke, but I remember a professor in seminary who could take one Greek word and spend a week explaining its complicated meaning. Yet he confessed that he could not come close to what the Biblical author really had in mind. On this humbling note, I never attempt to preach from the text itself without proper research. Another good idea is to consult one's fellow clergy, if you are in a staff situation. Chat about the text, have a bull session, and see what is stimulated in you about your chosen piece of scripture.

The second thing a passage will do for me, when I am sufficiently involved in it, is to help me think inwardly about my own faith. What does this text mean to me? How do I identify with the piece of writing or the author? What stirs in my imagination when I am confronted not just by the words of Matthew, Paul, or Luke, but more so by their lives, their own faith, their working out of their destinies under God?

The third aspect of the text method is that it can help me to unite the meaning of its contents with what is happening in the world today. The preacher is the catalyst that makes Scripture understandable. We all try to help others make sense of the world, to help them see that "love is at the heart of things," and not hate or indifference, or faceless, impersonal power. How does this text relate to the real world? It does relate, and always will—depending on the preacher's serious intention to live with the text for a few days or even hours before writing. I generally, but not always, read the text a day before I begin writing, just to see if some spark occurs, some little fire of "connectiveness" with life as most people understand it.

The theological basis for preparing a sermon from a text is, as I have said, one which keeps faith with the words of those persons who witnessed in Biblical times. By remaining as faithful as possible to the original intention of the text, one hopes that the "words in the Word of God" may break through the research and soul-searching that go into creating the sermon. The textual method keeps faith with Scripture more than with a current piece of literature, more than with a given pastoral situation, and is not primarily stimulated by conflict with the passage. I identify this method as utilizing a theology of transcendence and of emphasizing the Word of God as a variable, but also timeless, truth which is revealed in Holy Scripture. I do not mean timeless as "wooden," because Scriptural truth is not wooden. As someone has written, our task is not to change the Christian Faith to accommodate the world, but to relate the Christian faith to the world, and to stimulate in our listeners an appreciation for what is beyond the secular, the "this age" type of mentality which moderns always assume too readily. One of the fundamental questions of modern man is, "Is there anything more than the empirical evidence of life around me?" Is there another life, a life of the Spirit, a Kingdom or reign of God, a Heaven? The text method tries to tell the sacred story of our faith through Scripture first, then the preacher's own thought processes, cultural sources, conflict, and pastoral situation.

Sermon Number One

NOW OR ELSE

Hosanna to the Son of David.—Matthew 21

Palm Sunday is a day to say hosanna as an acclamation of triumph, but it is not the last word for Jesus this week. Soon hosannas said by the crowd will become only appeals to "crucify him." Both New Testament lessons this morning illustrate the full meaning of Holy Week. The first, which began the liturgy of the palms, contains Matthew's version of the triumphant entry into Jerusalem, and the second, the long account narrated so well by Mr. Wardwell, describes the process of rejection which leads to Jesus' trial and execution.

A little research tells us that the word "hosanna" is taken

from Psalm 118 and was recited ritually at annual festivals. While later used as a general cry of praise, the Hebrew word's original meaning is "save us now." Matthew adds to the word the phrase "To the Son of David." Thus the crowd in his Gospel is seen as acknowledging Jesus as the Messiah while the whole city becomes wild with excitement—a festival pilgrimage turned into a messianic demonstration.

But Matthew later writes of the realistic consequences of a messiahship rooted in prophetic expectation. Jesus is, as the Old Testament lesson from Isaiah states, a servant who bore our sufferings. "We despised him," "We held him of no account." He was wounded for our transgressions, "Chastized for our iniquities," and "The Lord laid on him the guilt of us all." Matthew is a firm believer in Jesus as this suffering servant and he writes like one. Don't expect him to have done otherwise, although his writing always allows us to draw our own conclusions. Unlike some contemporary evangelists, he offers us the freedom to doubt.

But the crowd resists such a Messiah: The ecstatic mood revealed in the cry, "hosanna," save us now, changes radically to cynical yells of "crucify him." How fickle we are. The contrast in cries highlights for us our own human tendency to say, *"now or else."* Save us now or we forget you, help us now or we "write you off," as if you were of no account, as if you had lost all likeness of being human, "your beauty changed beyond human semblance."

We know too well that many of the triumphs we hope for in life are never realized because our expectations are not on a level with actual possibilities. When the help we receive is not the kind we expect and it comes to us in a different guise than we anticipate, we often reject it. Then anger or depression results.

I think much of the disappointment which that crowd felt because of Jesus of Nazareth is due to the same natural and human misconceptions we also share about the meaning of life and of hope. For most of us he still fulfills the wrong prophecies, those which incorporate humility, pain, sorrow, loss, frustration, and hesitant decision-making—such as in the Garden of Gethsemane—and not enough of those attributes which belong to a strong authority figure who is seemingly always right, who will take care of us. We are always dangerously near totalitarianism. We are too easily tempted to sell our freedom, as Dostoevski reminds us through the Grand Inquisitor in *The Brothers Karamazov,* for bread. We leap from Palm Sunday to Easter and ignore Good Friday, and yet it is always the passion of Christ which helps us to understand and withstand life in its fullness.

Allow me to share with you a story about some friends of long ago who have had a difficult time. When I was a vicar of a small church in the Salinas Valley in California in 1959 I became acquainted with many young ranch families. They were a type of private mission ground which provided growth for the parish.

Most had gone to universities and had returned to the land of their fathers and mothers to carry on the work of large estates. One young family had three children, and after a normal bout with the flu, the youngest boy became listless for too long and was unable to regain any of his normal energy. He was taken to the doctor again and it was discovered that his white blood cell count was abnormally high and his illness was eventually diagnosed as leukemia. He was nine years old, and I will never forget him . . . he was a brave little boy. There were trying days ahead for his family, as you may well imagine, and, while both were broken-hearted, they were initially hopeful, especially the father, because new drugs—which now cluster under the name chemotherapy—were going to be used. The little boy did respond for a while and he did go into remission, but less than a year later he weakened and was placed in a hospital for the last time. Amazingly, the mother became stronger, but the father fell completely apart; his whole attitude turned to one of bitterness.

When the boy finally died, peacefully in his sleep one day, I was with the mother. The father, however, could not go near the hospital. After the burial he rejected his wife and family. While we cannot presume to know how any one of us would act in such a tragedy, it seemed to him that the loss of the boy was a personal insult because his death was something he could not control: it was beyond him; in spite of his strong outward bearing, he was unprepared to accept the same mysteries of life to which all of us are subject.

It seems—and I cite this example to inspire your compassion for them both—that when we expect "save us now," almost demand it from God or our loved ones, and do not receive the help we expect—as children often make unrealistic demands to test us—we too become like the crowd and say, "Crucify him" in bitter disappointment. Holy Week is a mirror by which to see ourselves; it is also God's way to help us come to grips with ourselves.

Palm Sunday without Good Friday is full of wishful thinking. Jesus rides into the midst of a happy and hopeful festival, his disciples help him by finding a little donkey for him to ride, excited citizens prepare his way by throwing palm branches or tree limbs in his path, carpeting the road in front of him as if he were some approaching king or conqueror—another David. Even Matthew succumbs to the temptation of the moment, and calls him "Son of David," but Jesus is as far removed from David as Mahatma Gandhi was from Peter the Great.

True religion includes the reality of the cross. First the worst, then the best; first anxiety, then calm; first the ability to confess brokenness, then healing. When we offer our inadequacies in our worship, which is a way of accepting them, we are often surprised by grace, and these palm branches indeed do mean then that Christ is our king. But follow him all the way, then sing his praises. Don't sing them too soon, lest you be broken-hearted, lest your own human need be unexpressed and your spirit filled with emptiness. Be a participant in Holy Week. Let this passion narrative sink into your soul, for it is your salvation. When we say of Jesus, "By his scourging we are healed, by his death we have gained life," then we begin to know what hope really is, then we cry "hosanna" as a festival shout, then we no longer defiantly say "now or else," but "whenever, Lord, and thanks."

The king does come in glory when we have accepted the king's cross, when we have taken it and hoisted it on our backs, and after realizing that we are not broken by it, when we see that indeed we can carry it—because somehow by God's grace we know that he is really carrying it for us and we are not alone—then any day can become a Palm Sunday and every day is an Easter.

Personal Record and Discussion of Sermon

Sources of Inspiration

The textual sermon for me is the most difficult for it demands that I restrict myself to Scripture alone for inspiration, that I place it above all other secondary sources of inspiration. When I viewed this text, Matthew 21, and meditated on its meaning, particularly "Hosanna to the Son of David" from the entrance of Jesus into Jerusalem on Palm Sunday, I was confronted by all the busy activities of Holy Week. I felt overwhelmed, as if too much were expected of me. When this happens I usually become a little depressed and worried for fear that I will not come up with the "big message." For some reason I remembered a story from my past about a boy who died at eight years of age in my first church in 1959. Perhaps I recalled that boy's family and their misery because we confront tragedy in Holy Week. Perhaps thinking ahead to the music of Easter made me think of that little boy who died of leukemia; because at his burial service long ago I used Hymn 91, "The strife is o'er, the battle done," a classic Easter hymn and a favorite of mine.

I also noticed the contrast in the two lessons for Palm Sunday, the one of the entry to the Holy City, exemplified by "Hosanna" and the other, the long Passion narrative which is read as the Gospel and which can be summed up by the word "crucify." I began to think how can I contrast the euphoria of Palm Sunday with the terror of Good Friday, and thus proceeded to write.

Choice of Method

I chose the text method because Scripture and tradition present the story of Holy Week, and my task was to represent the reality of Jesus' last days on earth and apply that reality to our lives.

Intention of Sermon

My intention was to contrast Palm Sunday with Good Friday and to help my listeners understand that there is no easy Easter. I wanted Palm Sunday and Good Friday to become real existentially, a little like I believe Bultmann tried to do in his preaching. I hoped to transform Sunday and Friday into almost personal events which can inform our faith and help us to understand life and its problems.

Personal Record

Sermons come to me in two main ways: one as a free brainstorming method of typewriting in my office, or in the middle of the night by hand on a yellow pad. On Tuesday I began because the organist and I chose the hymns and double-checked the lessons in the lectionary, especially when options are offered. This sermon presented me with a dilemma. On the one hand, at a busy time, I had to get started and to "hack it out," like a newspaper reporter who has a deadline; on the other, I struggled to be creative, to tie Scripture to reality, to make the Word of God become the word for men and women. Something in me did happen, does in most sermons, which is like two wires crossing each other to produce a spark, even a jolt. That spark is what transforms "hacking it out" into being innovative, and it is difficult to achieve after preaching on Palm Sunday for twenty years.

To be truthful this sermon came to me at 3:00 A.M. and I wrote my first draft. Then on Wednesday I typed it up, on Thursday after making home calls I typed another draft, finishing it properly on Friday morning in time for the secretary to type a finished copy in large letters. I played with it on Saturday, and then retyped most of it myself again on Saturday afternoon.

Documentation of Sources

a. Matthew 21, Psalm 118, Isaiah 52
b. Harvey, A. E., *Companion to the New Testament*

c. *Interpreter's Bible*, Volumes 4, 5, 7

d. Dostoevski, F., *The Brothers Karamazov*

Number of Drafts and Time Taken

Four drafts, twenty-one hours

Last Minute Changes of Thought

I hit upon "Now or Else" as a title late and used "Save us now or we forget you, help us now or we write you off, as if you were of no account, as if you had lost all likeness of being human" at the end of my rewriting. I boldly used "We are always dangerously near totalitarianism" at the last minute, interjecting Dostoevski. Reality seemed summed up to me in these sentences: "But follow him all the way, then sing his praises. Don't sing them too soon, lest you be broken-hearted, lest your own human need be unexpressed and your spirit filled with emptiness." These were not so much last minute changes as "refinements."

Possible Revision of Intention

My intention remained the same at the end as in the beginning in this particular sermon.

Hearing Group's Response

N.P. "A minister's basic job is to interpret the Scripture and Ernie did that very well today. In addition, it is the minister's job to bring comfort (in the sense of strength) and he did that too. But I was left with no clear grasp of the basic point."

J.N. "As I listened I asked myself, what am I getting out of this? and I realized that I needed the reminder of the Passion, rather than keeping my focus just on Easter." She said of the story of the dying child that she felt she would be like the father. [Later she said she felt the story not really appropriate.]

N.P. and J.N. Both felt this sermon not as inspired and successful as your sermons usually are, no clear ringing note, but comforting.

J.N.   "On the other hand, I found myself thinking I just might go to the Good Friday service (for the first time) so maybe I got more out of it than I realized."

J.K.   "I responded mainly to your point that we should not have unrealistic expectations. I am sure it is because I had such expectations that the holocaust was able to drive me away from the church for so long—instead of *to* it as would have been appropriate."

Sermon Number Two

EMPTY TOMBS: FULL LIVES

But God raised Him on the third day and made Him manifest.
                                                           —Acts 10

Easter begins with an empty tomb but is soon witnessed to by convinced and prayerful believers who have learned that empty tombs mean full lives.

The abrupt ending of St. Mark's Gospel, which some believe to be unfinished, moves from concern about the stone in front of a tomb to the discovery of an empty tomb, to a statement, "He is risen, He is not here," to an immediate and quite human response of fear in the face of mystery. In the other Gospels the appearances occur thereafter until a firm belief emerges in the community of survivors, the church, that Jesus has been uniquely raised up from death by God. But in the Book of Acts, particularly in the reading today, its author, St. Luke, puts into Peter's speech devotional, almost prayerlike phrases which reveal the young church's resurrection faith.

Yet it is necessary to make quite clear from the very beginning, especially on Easter Sunday, that it was not just Jesus' message which the disciples kept alive. They did not see themselves filling in for him, so to speak, because he had died. They were not merely preaching his cause. We are tempted to understand resurrection as our power, rather than God's power, because we sometimes revere leaders filled with charisma who have been assassinated. We listen to their words or see them again on television and then we carry on their good work, but this is not what happened to the followers of Jesus.

As Hans Küng writes: "His cause was not enough by itself, it is the question of the living person and therefore the cause." What the disciples had given up on as lost was decided at Easter by God himself. He does not live because he is proclaimed, but he is proclaimed because he lives. Thus Christians know of an empty tomb, filled at first by men, but emptied by God. We preach resurrection, not revolution as divine justice.

Empty tombs are meant for full lives, however. They push us into a confrontation with ultimate mystery; they remind us that Easter is the only source of strength for the church.

He is proclaimed because he lives. Without this proclamation we have nothing to offer. With it we can be as convinced as Peter, who said, "We are witnesses . . . they put him to death by hanging him on a tree" but God raised him on the third day and made him manifest.

Such conviction informs our actions today. For example, two years ago this last Ash Wednesday I promised that the clergy of this parish would pray for Archbishop Janani Luwum of Uganda until persecution of Christians by Amin ceased. Archbishop Luwum, who had then recently earned a doctorate from Oxford, was one of Africa's leading scholars and gentle Christians, and yet General Amin dragged Janani before a crowd and personally accused him of being a traitor and blasphemer. "This is the judgment of God," Amin said to the press. Dressed in his bishop's purple robe, as was Jesus similarly dressed in mockery on Good Friday, Luwum heard the people yell, "kill him, kill him," which to a Christian is always the hideous cry of "crucify, crucify." The church is catholic—what happens in one part of it affects another: we could do no less than to remember him in our prayers even if we had to mention his name indefinitely.

Janani (John) Luwum was the third archbishop of the Anglican Communion to be martyred: the first was Thomas à Becket by soldiers of Henry II, the second was Archbishop Thomas Cranmer under the reign of Queen Mary, and then a

Black Becket, whose death occurred in a country which has more Anglicans than we have Episcopalians in North America. Tertullian wrote that the blood of the martyrs is the seed of the church.

When a Christian is martyred, an African Christian wrote, "tremendous things begin to happen." Our prayers in church are not just exercises in personal fulfillment: they are devotional actions which manifest our Easter faith. Prayer for a martyr is more than a way to say, "We will not forget," but to state firmly, "Christ will overcome this evil as he did the cross."

For two years we have prayed at one of our Sunday services and thus we have kept public in a small way what governments and newspapers too soon forget, that perhaps 300,000 Ugandans were still victims and that a great injustice had been committed. We did so because we are members of the whole church and because we believe God is faithful.

We have not prayed for Luwum's cause, however. He did not have any doctrine, only his concern for his people. We have not prayed that Amin be overthrown, even though it appears now that he is finished as a dictator. We have prayed for the soul of Luwum, which is quite different and could not be a reality for us if we did not believe that he is with God as you and I will be with the Father, because of Easter. Without this day we could not turn anger into prayer; we would be left only the legacy of a Good Friday, of a tragedy: then we could hope only in revolution, but revolution is not resurrection. Marxism may proclaim that a good end can justify an evil means, and therefore a violent cataclysmic overthrow can also be justified, which is nothing new in history: an eye for an eye, a murder for a murder, an Amin for a Luwum. But the church's way, when it is true to itself, is based on emptying tombs, not in filling more of them.

On Easter two years ago our presiding bishop asked each of us to mail Easter cards to every Christian we knew in Uganda, and because one Sunday Associate under Dr. McCandless had become the bishop of a diocese in Uganda, we mailed our cards to him. We understand that the post office in Kampala was flooded with simple messages of hope, of joy, of faith. One could hardly call this revolutionary, but it meant that the church is tenacious and that we care. There is a kind of power in patient witness, which demands more from us than anger hastily expressed in some act of violence. We wait and pray, not as those who are weak, but as those who believe in the ultimate moral purpose of history.

Such was the witness of the apostles. Resurrection is the power of all just men and women unjustly executed being justified by God in time. We are not left alone in our tragedies because God is a redeemer of unjust deeds. We sing of victories of the spirit today, and not of ultimate defeat, even beyond the grave.

God does vindicate, but not primarily through human violence. The day of Yahweh, which in the Old Testament often meant a day of vengeance against the enemies of Israel or a day of retribution for the sins of Israel, a manifestation of God's righteousness, is transformed for us in the light of Easter. It becomes not an occasion of vengeance but of rebirth and renewal.

Nicolas Berdyaev once wrote: "The whole of the world must be made to pass through death and resurrection, else it cannot attain resurrection and eternity." Easter is for us the meaning to history as well as to eternity, the meaning to life as well as to death. We have been given the example of one who overcame the grave. "Because he lives he is proclaimed." Because he lives we are able to pray for those who have died and thus for justice from God: we can even afford to pray for our enemies.

Empty tombs are symbols for full lives, for hope after human injustice because God is faithful—that is why we are joyous today, why we celebrate this day, this Easter.

Personal Record and Discussion of Sermon

Sources of Inspiration

I first began digesting the text of the Resurrection narrative in St. Mark's Gospel because this was to be an Easter sermon and because the church lectionary this year used cycle "B." The Gospel of Mark was read throughout the year. But I soon changed to the reading from Acts in which St. Peter delivers a resurrection sermon. However, both texts were in my mind. I tried to be honest about Peter's speech, that it essentially was a way for St. Luke to confess his faith, or the faith of the early church. The then-current situation in Uganda, in which it seemed that Idi Amin's regime would soon fall and that the suffering of that country, and its Christians, would soon come to an end, spurred me on to use Uganda as a concrete and meaningful way to speak of God's justice and of his ultimate justice, the Resurrection.

I found some old notes I had made on the Resurrection from Hans Küng's *On Being a Christian,* and was seized by a sense of boldness from the words of Peter. Küng's "He is proclaimed because He lives," seemed in proper keeping to Luke's faith, and at the same time I remembered Berdyaev's emphasis that resurrection is for history as well as eternity. This sermon was theological, that is, I used it to state my faith.

Choice of Method

I chose the "textual method" because of Easter, and because the narrative revealed the basis for the early church's faith and our faith.

Intention of Sermon

My intention was to preach the Good News of Resurrection as more than a matter of immanence, as the evidence of our human aspirations of nature. It is, at least to me, a transcendent reality. In my mind I associated resurrection with all justice, with divine justice, and with the joyous news of the coming justice in Uganda. Since we had two visits by exiled Bishop Kivengere of Uganda and one of our Sunday assistants in the past had become Bishop of Buganda, a province of that country, and had gone through much persecution, I decided to use Uganda as the living example of God's promises fulfilled.

Personal Record

On Tuesday I began to take notes and then I "brainstormed" as usual on my typewriter, that is, I produced five pages of information and insights without organization of thought. I consulted commentaries from the beginning and came to some additional conclusions. Then on Wednesday, I typed another draft and was unhappy about it. I had begun to worry about Good Friday and let my draft for Easter sit on my desk. On Thursday I worked on my Good Friday meditation, and then Thursday night I came down with a very bad case of the stomach virus, which others in the parish also had, and on Good Friday during the three-hour service I delivered my meditation in poor, although not too evident, sick condition.

Then Friday night and Saturday I reworked the second draft, and late on Saturday I retyped it in large print in the secretary's office. My wife had gone to our house in the country on Thursday, and I planned to join her on Sunday afternoon. From long experience she knows that Good Friday and Easter are very traumatic times for me.

In the beginning, as I have stated, I had a difficult time choosing the text, because I could not find enough inspiration in one or the other. Finally I settled on Acts and in honesty said, "But in the Book of Acts . . . its author, St. Luke, puts into Peter's speech devotional, almost prayer-like phrases which reveal the young church's resurrection faith." I cited Hans Küng and later Berdyaev. A key phrase was "Resurrection is the power of all just men and women unjustly executed being justified by God in time."

Although resurrection to me is a reality of everyday life, in the sense that crucifixion and resurrection help us to understand ourselves and the nature of human existence, I wanted this sermon to be properly anchored in Scripture.

Documentation of Sources

  a. St. Mark 16:1–8
  b. The Book of Acts 10:34–43
  c. Harvey, A. E., *Companion to the New Testament*
  d. *Interpreter's Bible*, Volumes 7 and 9

Number of Drafts and Time Taken

Four drafts, fifteen hours

Last Minute Changes of Thought

My intention remained the same: to preach the Resurrection as a transcendent power which renews history and provides us with eternity.

Possible Revision of Intention

Switching texts occurred late in the week. I was assisted at that time by discovering an old Ash Wednesday meditation which referred to Archbishop Luwum's death in Uganda. This material provided the basis for a real-life situation for my preaching.

Hearing Group's Response

J.N.   Said she had forgotten we were to evaluate today so listened without any conscious intent to react. She said she felt you had put together the best of all the previous sermons—in your own reaction to the committee's comments.

N.P.   I should have noted before the above that I saw Nate Pusey just as he and Anne were leaving, hurriedly, for Connecticut. He thought the sermon splendid; he gave it "high marks."

S.B.   Found the sermon uplifting and positive but was not sure what the message was.

J.N.   Thought that the part on martyrdom was excellent.

S.B.   Agreed, but did not see the connection between martyrdom and the rest of the sermon.

W.B.   Also said he missed the usual laser-like quality.

S.B.   Liked the image of empty tombs/full lives, but, again, did not see any connections.

W.B.   Same kind of remarks as Susan's—the emphasis on Christian tenacity.

J.N. Liked the emphasis on the role of martyrs and on the importance of resurrection.

S.B. Tried to recall a structure of thought crucial and had wanted to hear more—it apparently had to do with God's faithfulness.

J.K. "I said at this point that what had come through most clearly to me was a sense of the strength of the Christian involvement and that that message made me feel strong, too." The others agreed that had been an important element in the sermon for them.

W. & S.B. Liked the emphasis on the fact that Christ lives on because of his resurrection—that we proclaim him because he lives.

J.N. Agreed and said that we all say he was raised but you made it actual.

W.B. Noted that we each had responded to different aspects of the sermon and perhaps it was by design that there was not one clear point—that you had wanted to create a mosaic of impressions and had succeeded very well.

S.B. "For all my confusion in trying to find one clear point I nonetheless am glad this was not the usual Easter sermon. This was obviously one thing Ernie wanted to say because it was important to him."

J.N. "Ernie stood there like a *leader*—he was very good."

[The others agreed.]

J.K. "When I reread this, I realized that some of it may make the reaction sound negative when I do not think it was. They were obviously excited by the sermon, speaking rapidly, interrupting each other, liking the sermon, but to some extent, searching for the reason why!"

Sermon Number Three

REPENTANCE AND REJOICING

Repentance is associated with joy, not judgment, in this morning's gospel, "There is rejoicing in heaven over one sinner who repents." Jesus did not identify penitence with guilt as much as with inward spiritual discovery, with looking honestly and deeply into the mirror of human existence and seeing that we are less than whole without an ultimacy beyond ourselves. Finding that God forgives and embraces us is to come to truth like lost sheep who are found, wandering prodigals who return home, prayerful publicans who cry for mercy rather than claim righteousness. Repentance therefore transcends the human level and has ultimate repercussions.

But this "fellow" Jesus, they said, welcomes sinners and eats with them. Jesus did not ask people to repent before he sat down at their table, even before they joined his company. In fact, it appears that Jesus sought out those considered outside the law, and spent much of his time with them, even while there was evidently an elitist element in the popular religion of his day which had a tendency to exclude anyone whose way of life or whose profession was different. Jesus was criticized for his actions.

So have been some of the striking workers in Poland. One of the demands of working men and women there, as you know, has been the elimination of special class treatment for communist party officials, an elite group in each of the Warsaw Pact countries. These strikers, certainly not living in any worker's paradise, simply wanted the rights of most unionists in the Western World as well as not to be treated as second-class citizens.

Jesus reacted the same way to the religion of his day. That special religious group called the Pharisees, who often challenged Jesus' openness to those without privilege, also believed in repentance, best translated as "the striking worker should go back to work immediately!" On this basis, penitents would be accepted by God, but it was essential in the Pharisees' minds that "sinners," or their version of outsiders and wrongdoers, must take the initiative themselves. Only then could they be welcomed by God, which sounds reasonable enough. The Pharisees were above all reasonable men. No wonder they couldn't fathom Jesus. His vision was not about reasonable behavior but about an individual's personal discovery of the Kingdom of God in his life.

In Luke's version of this New Testament text, the shepherd lifts the sheep onto his shoulders (the only way of carrying an injured or exhausted animal) and the poor woman invites friends and neighbors in to celebrate her rediscovery of a measly $2.42 worth of silver pieces. All the emphasis of this text is on the joy of what follows finding something which was lost. Repentance therefore is more than making amends, it triggers joy in heaven like ripples along an infinite sea.

Luke's Messiah welcomes sinners and restores the poor. It is terrifying to lose something precious in life, to have hope and then see it crushed. Even the simple act of losing one's wallet or a set of keys can disorient us and change the normality of our lives. I was mugged once; I know what it feels like to lose one's identity through theft. I lost all my keys one morning in suburban St. Louis when my 86-year-old grandmother, who lived with us, was at my side. I remember that she asked me to find something she had placed in the garage, and in doing so I put my keys down somewhere, locking both of us out of the house, car, and church, the three main foci of my existence. I felt quite ridiculous and even a little helpless. That morning I was supposed to open the church, to which I had to drive my car first, and my nearly deaf grandmother, tugging at my elbow to go back into the house, treated me as if I were some ogre who wanted her to remain shivering in the morning cold. I looked and looked, and after what seemed an eon of time, but in reality was probably just a few minutes, I discovered my precious keys in an obscure corner of the garage, quite well hidden under some boxes. To see those keys shine in their little hiding place was a sight joyous to behold. I felt restored and normal again. I could carry on my responsibilities on time.

No one likes to be locked out, whether "sinners" in Jesus' day or workers in Poland. Everyone wants access to the life they believe is possible, and when that life is realized or restored there is joy and celebration. Finding God as loving ultimacy is like discovering one's true happiness.

In that former parish of mine in St. Louis was a modern tapestry hanging on the wall of the nave. A shepherd was portrayed carrying a black sheep over his shoulders while the other white sheep looked on; it was the lost lamb of God which the shepherd had found and was carrying. The church's task is to seek those outside it, to proclaim that repentance celebrates our individuality in God. In Christianity one person is worth more than all the masses, in fact the masses in the gospel are never called the masses but the multitudes.

Multitudes of people live in this city but it is difficult to find warmth in them. Many are out of touch with genuine supportive love. We distance ourselves from each other, sometimes from necessity, but the price is often hostility, suspicion, and a lack of community. Carl Jung once wrote:

> No inferior form of energy can be simply converted into a superior form unless at the same time a source of higher value lends its support.

It was the Roman Catholic Church (and Pope John Paul II) which lent ultimate support to the worker's struggle in Poland, and at its best our church is capable of doing the same for each of us. Even though we fail, we have tried to take the initiative, to be lay and clergy shepherds who carry the injured in spirit into union with the 99 who have been restored.

The contrast between waiting for those outside to take the initiative and our initiative is the point of this text. God takes the initiative in loving us; we are loved even before we begin to love. He does not wait for us to be good, but rather acts when we have a vision of the way things can be. Then in union with his support change occurs in us and in society, and we celebrate our new selves and our new situations.

There is joy in heaven for one Polish worker who takes the initiative to strike; there is joy in heaven for one city dweller who finds an open space within himself which only a loving, shepherding God can fill. This text is all about each of us. "We are pieces of silver," St. Ambrose wrote. "Let us jealously cherish our value!" Repentance is about joy and finding our worth which derives ultimately from the God and Father of our Lord and Savior Jesus Christ.

Personal Record and Discussion of Sermon

Sources of Inspiration

This sermon was the first preached after a month's vacation, and I found it difficult to come back to the task of writing a sermon. I discovered that the text from the lectionary was St. Luke 15:1–10, the story of Jesus who welcomes tax-gatherers, tells the story of the lost sheep, and also of the woman who loses a silver piece. The theme in this passage is well stated in the line, "There will be greater joy in heaven over one sinner who repents. . . ." Believing that it is more difficult for many people to associate repentance with joy than with guilt and restitution, I consulted several commentaries to see how I could make this text "live," that is, be discovered as true and authentic as it applied to their lives and to the world. Luke's Messiah welcomes sinners and restores the poor; "Jesus did not ask people to repent before he sat down at their table, even before they joined his company," I eventually wrote.

I suppose one source of inspiration for me was my own reaction to the text in the light of my personal history. Everyone wrestles with guilt, and we fall into the trap of believing that we are accepted only after we do something about our selves, our sins, our maturity to grow in certain areas. But the text indicates we are accepted by God all along. I finally wrote: "Finding that God forgives and embraces us is to come to truth like lost sheep who are found, wandering prodigals who return home, prayerful publicans who cry for mercy rather than claim righteousness." The text was the primary source of inspiration.

Choice of Method

Since I had little conflict with this text, in fact found it to be liberating, I chose to begin with text, work through "cultural sources" and "conflict" to the "pastoral situation."

Intention of Sermon

My original intention was to help my listeners to discover the "joy" referred to in the text and to have repentance seen in the context of being found and of finding God.

Personal Record

I got off to a slow start after the Labor Day weekend and couldn't really begin my sermon until Wednesday, when I went over the hymns with our organist, reviewing the lectionary together. The lectionary in The Book of Common Prayer is divided into three-year cycles, A,B,C and this was year "C," with prescribed Old Testament, Epistle, and Gospel lessons for "Proper 19," the Sunday nearest the one for which I had to preach. I always try to preach from the lessons; indeed we publish them a week before in our leaflet so that some members of the congregation may read them before attending services.

The recent Polish conflict in which "Solidarity" had gone on strike was on my mind, in fact I had saved several newspaper articles about it on vacation. I thought that identifying "elimination of special class treatment for communist party officials" by the Polish strikers with the elitist religious attitude of those who accused Jesus of welcoming sinners would help illuminate the text. I purposefully made a comparison between Pharisees and the communist elite, and then wrote that repentance according to a Pharisee might be equated with "the striking worker should go back to work immediately!" just as Pharisees believed sinners had to take the initiative with God—which sounds reasonable enough.

Then I moved on to thinking (and later writing), "The Pharisees were above all reasonable men," but Jesus' "vision was not about reasonable behavior but about an individual's personal discovery of the Kingdom of God in his life." Most of these thoughts I wrote down on a pad, which I took home Wednesday night to complete after dinner. To be sure, after reviewing what I had written, and after rereading the end section of the text about the woman who lost her silver coin, another idea came to me to help explain the passage. I remembered my 86-year-old Welsh grandmother and the time I was locked out of my house, church, and car, and I wove that event into my sermon, writing: "no one likes to be locked out, whether 'sinners' in Jesus' day or workers in Poland."

The next day I typed a draft in my office, adding a story from my former parish and a quote from Carl Jung, which seemed to lend support to my claim that "the church's task is to seek those outside it, to proclaim that repentance celebrates our individuality in God." On Friday morning I typed another draft, comparing in the conclusion a Polish worker with a city dweller, with sinners who repent and create joy in heaven. My secretary typed the final draft in the afternoon.

Documentation of Sources

a. The Gospel of St. Luke 15:1–10
b. Harvey, A. E., *Companion to the New English Bible*
c. Wirt, Sherwood, editor, *Living Quotations for Christians*, Harper and Row, N.Y., 1974, p. 43
d. Toal, M. F., editor, *The Sunday Sermons of the Great Fathers*, Vol. III, Henry Regnery Company, Chicago, 1964, p. 196

Number of Drafts and Time Taken

Four drafts, eighteen hours

Last Minute Changes of Thought

I remembered a quotation from St. Ambrose in a collection of sermons of the Fathers which I keep on my desk, and I thought it appropriate to add to my conclusion. "We are pieces of silver . . . let us jealously cherish our value," Ambrose preached, which fit in nicely with the woman who lost her coin and my final emphasis that "repentance is about joy and finding our worth which derives ultimately from the God and Father of our Lord and Savior Jesus Christ." I added this quotation later on Saturday, writing it into the typed text.

Possible Revision of Intention

My intention changed somewhat as I ended this sermon. I added to my original purpose the theme of "individuality," in contrast to the masses (as seen in a deterministic view of history) which seemed to heighten the importance of repentance. Repentance implies a change of heart or free choice, which in turn suggests "our value" as "pieces of silver" to God. So I added "repentance celebrates our individuality in God."

4

The Cultural Sources Method

The second method is one which begins from some "cultural source," that is, literature, artful quotations, newspaper articles, sociological statements, psychology, or any source other than Holy Scripture. The springboard here is not analysis of the text, and the way the text becomes personally meaningful—although the text is included—but rather a book one has been reading and perhaps the faith, or lack of faith, of the author. For example, several years ago I read a book which seemed so vital to me that I took about twenty-five pages of notes. That book was *Lyrical and Critical Essays,* by Albert Camus. I have his words, rather than the words of Scripture, to stimulate and inspire me. Being something of an existentialist, I like to ponder the meaning of human existence. Life does often seem absurd.

Camus ruminates in these essays about the meaning of tragedy for the post-World War II European world, and his insights are invaluable to me. They inspired me. Sometimes the hymn which may become the sermon hymn for the Sunday I preach is so full of truth that I am stimulated to preach from its words. In the Hymnal 1940 of the Episcopal Church there are many good hymns which need explaining, or can provide a basis for influencing the preacher to write his sermon. One new hymn, which is known to some in the church, begins "My song is Love unknown," and continues, "My Savior's love to me, / Love to the loveless shown, / That they might lovely be. / O Who am I / That for my sake / My Lord should take / Frail flesh and die." The theological truth in these words is like an unmined cavern, fresh and ready for digging, for discovering of precious spiritual metals, for unknown treasures of the Spirit. How many sermons could be entitled, "Love to the Loveless Shown."

Recently I read *Towards the Mountain,* the first part of an autobiography of Alan Paton, the South African Anglican writer whose witness against apartheid has been consistent for almost a lifetime. His analysis of the history of South Africa as well as his place in it, and his own faith, presents a rich source of inspiration for the sermon writer. I always take notes when I read anything which borders on theological truth, or an accurate assessment of the human condition. And another favorite book is Graham Greene's *Power and the Glory,* or more recently his *Ways of Escape* in which he tells why and how he wrote his books, or where he was most influenced to write them—and he has traveled widely.

Travel itself stimulates us, a change of location; or poetry, perhaps a motion picture, can induce us to write. I referred recently to "Breaker Morant," a motion picture about Australians fighting the Boer War for the "Empire," who on orders kill prisoners and yet are convicted by a courtmartial to death for doing so. Even *Psychology Today,* a sort of pop psychology glossy magazine, has articles or interviews which can give us courage to begin a sermon.

Personally I do not keep a systematic file on 5-by-8 cards of "cultural sources" as I understand some preachers do. But since my experience has been as a writing contributor to a monthly periodical based on newspaper articles from a South American country, I clip articles, take notes, and stack them in a file box for future use. Luckily, my memory is good enough to recall that I did save a particular article, or five sheets of quotations from such and such a source; and I am able to dig them up for reference when needed.

The theology of beginning from a piece of literature or from the newspaper does imply that I believe that God is at work in the world, that we are to look for signs of his Holy Spirit everywhere. He is not confined to the church; his Spirit is free and rests on all, but we Christians have the responsibility, not the privilege, of being able to see the signs of his activity through men and women of good will and their works. And so, for convenience, I identify this method as more concerned with "immanence," with natural theology and revelation, with God at work in the lives of all people—whether they appreciate it or not, whether they are faithful or not, whether they believe or not. God is not bound by human sin, nor is he intimidated by the good or bad behavior of the professed unbeliever. He loves and works through all, and it is for us to be supportive enough, as well as critical enough, of those sources outside Scripture in order for them to become the Word of God in our sermons.

In this method I certainly do not intend to deny "transcendence" but to affirm "immanence," to say that as a Scripturally-oriented, willing captive of the institutional, organized church, I eagerly seek divine truth, and affirmation of Scripture and of church, in the words and works of those sometimes at war with Holy Writ or outside the church. In any case, this "cultural sources" chapter offers three sermons as examples, a personal diary of how each was written, and a hearing response for two which were preached in a series specifically designed for lay feedback.

Sermon Number One

EXPANDED HORIZONS, NOT EXPANDED EGOS

Jesus does not call us to expanded egos but to expanded horizons. Trustee of Stanford University and former secretary of health, John Gardner, recently wrote:

You can win the world's adoring respect, perform legendary deeds, be anything, do anything . . . but no one mentions the force that most often rages for total freedom: the insatiable ego. In such an atmosphere, it's hardly surprising that we encounter individuals who nurse a deep grievance; life owes them something—if only some kind of recognition. . . . We are not very good at communicating to our children that life has always been hard and always will be, that the world was not designed for our personal enjoyment.

What then is the world designed for, if not for our personal pleasure? The New Testament text this morning gives us one answer. Contented perhaps, but limited persons find new strength for growth and conflict through faith. Jesus says, "Follow me and I will make you fishers of men." There is no long speech about the meaning of "call," no serious deliberation about who should be ordained or not, because Mark presents us with a time-frame which precedes that of the church, and its later concerns. Here we are in the living presence of the historical Jesus. Mark writes straightforwardly—not systematically as later Christians like Calvin or Barth, but as a narrator highlighting the enormous impact of the Messiah on him and others. He leaves much to our imagination, but we can elicit from the text a few conclusions.

Jesus challenged some persons to leave what they were doing and to follow his way. Those who responded positively (we do not know how many did not) left behind their natural setting and its implicit lifestyle; in this case, that which blends with a sea with beaches, a boat with sails, a net with fish. They were obviously tough persons who could haul in teeming nets and weather heavy storms. They were used to cleaning fish and perhaps bartering with some local broker or merchant for a fair price. They probably shared stories of great experiences in their boats and expanded their egos when they spoke of the size of the fish they had caught at sea. They were more than likely simple fisherfolk, contented and peaceful, as we sang in our hymn this morning, "before the Lord came down."

We do not know their personal reasons for accepting Jesus' invitation, but it is obvious they willingly did so. No fisherman off a wharf in San Francisco or out from the shore of Maine would leave a boat, a business, and a possible profit without compelling reasons. St. Mark, however, provides no evidence of a spectacular, legendary conversion experience—a sudden burst out of obscurity—but rather, a quiet decision to serve the Kingdom Jesus claimed was imminent and of ultimate importance.

There is a difference between an expanded ego and an expanded horizon. The first is caught up with itself; it does not center on *other* great possibilities. The latter, although more difficult to discern, is infinitely more important to the self in the long run. An expanded horizon helps us look beyond the sorrows and the shortcomings of the present to a hopeful future; it assists us to see things we would never see otherwise about ourselves and our world. It enables us to do things we never considered possible, and we are changed into persons we never thought we could or would become. Faith is a way to describe expanded horizons.

Part of following Christ is discovering that liberation without the ultimate view of faith can be a form of slavery, sometimes a reaction to the past alone, as if these fisherfolk were disgusted with fishing and the miserable smell of fish, "before the Lord came down," and were saved from it all. We do not sense any negativism in Mark's version of Jesus' call, but a positive, wordless, solid response to the "peace of God that filled their hearts brimful," and later, "broke them too." They would soon begin ministries of healing, forgiving, and teaching, and would have their hearts set on fire by miracles of God's love they would never fully understand, but "young John would die on Patmos, homeless," and Peter "head down was crucified. . . ."

Real freedom has its price. We pay for the insight of knowing that the meaning of life, of the earth, of the cosmos, is love defined by a cross. Yet our expanded horizon also looks beyond crucifixion to a Christ who continues to beckon followers after his resurrection. Even today he leads us into this Body of his and calls us, not to worry so much about how far a few loaves and fishes will go, but about God's love for all people, about the Kingdom of God and its possibilities, about the mission of the church and its needs—which leads me to speak to you of our situation here at the Epiphany.

Each year we remind ourselves of an "Expanded Horizon," especially on this Sunday in which we have our Annual Meeting. Last year we cut expenses and increased income without incurring any significant deficit. I know that each of you understands how difficult it is for a small parish in New York City to sustain a pastoral ministry and effective programs—a strong Sunday school, a stimulating adult forum, a growing young adult's group—through talented staff, without overexpenditure of funds. Program without deficit is a difficult tension to maintain and we may be the only parish doing such in this city. Yet our yearly challenge is to keep this church responding to the Kingdom while refusing to allow it to become a small barren place where nets lie idle and our boat is full of dry rot.

Speaking of dry rot, we face physical problems in this building, a tower which needs extensive repair, windows in that tower with holes in them which endanger the organ and could lead to enormous expense, temporary light fixtures since 1939 which are burning out and a light which no longer works. We face thousands of dollars worth of mending our nets here in the sure and certain hope that this building will continue to house a dynamic congregation. We are also challenged by "Venture in Mission," a call from above in which the national church, the diocese and some of the lay leadership of this parish ask us to support evangelism and help for the needy beyond our canvass—later after Easter.

While we have had a successful canvass, ably led this year, being a Christian and a churchman is not easy, and it has not been easy since Jesus first called Simon and John. We are a church which encourages participation. While only two of the clergy are fully employed here and one is part-time, we try to fill the sanctuary with both clergy and lay people. We have had a thirty-three year history of involving many people in worship, but this is because we are trying to have the most effective response possible to the highest responsibility given us all, to make each of us co-partners in worship so that we *can all together follow him.*

We do not desire the world's regard or recognition. To speak colloquially, we are not on an "ego trip" here, knowing too well that this world was not designed for our personal enjoyment. The world is a testing place of service to others, a place to draw us out of ourselves. It, to be sure, is a dying garden of Eden, but it is also always coming alive again through the Kingdom of God. The church communicates to it and to its children, expanded horizons, not expanded egos. "Come, follow me," Our Lord said, "and I will make you fishers of men." I will offer you a difficult but rewarding vision of unlimited possibilities.

"The peace of God, it is no peace. But strife closed in the sod. Yet brothers and sisters, pray for but one thing—the marvelous peace of God."

Personal Record and Discussion of Sermon

Sources of Inspiration
The following quotation from former Secretary of Health John Gardner stimulated my thinking about the meaning of service in relation to our own self-centered needs.

> You can win the world's adoring respect, perform legendary deeds, be anything . . . do anything . . . where expanded egos congregate there is much talk of liberation . . . but no one mentions the force that most often rages for total freedom: the insatiable ego. In such an atmosphere, it is hardly surprising that we encounter individuals who nurse a deep grievance; life owes them something—if only some kind of recognition. . . .

> We are not very good at communicating to our children that life has always been hard and always will be, that the world was not designed for our personal enjoyment.

When I thought of this piece in relation to the text from the New Testament lectionary for the day, "Follow me, and I will make you fishers of men," I seemed to have the ingredients for a sermon which would contrast self-fulfillment with service to others. Yet my hope was to help people understand that service to others, or Christian discipleship, is in fact a fulfillment. In the back of my mind was the fact that our parish annual meeting was going to be held immediately after the church service at 11:00 A.M., a meeting in which financial reports and selection of new vestrymembers would take place. In a way a sermon in our parish on this day is a type of keynote address in which I challenge the church for the year ahead and present some of our parish needs.

Choice of Method

I chose the Gardner quotation as a source and consciously moved from it to the text, into areas of conflict and pastoral consideration. I used the "cultural source" method.

Intention of Sermon

My intention was to speak to discipleship on a personal basis as well as to address the financial and physical needs of our church in the new year. Yet if a stranger walked into our service and knew nothing about annual meetings or falling glass from the tower of the church, I hoped he or she would gain something from my words for his or her own spiritual growth. The line from the sermon, "Contented but perhaps limited persons find new strength for growth and conflict through faith," was a key sentence in applying the sermon to each individual.

Personal Record

Gardner's words stimulated me to think of the contrast to "expanded egos," by referring to "expanded horizons." Most of my own creativity comes through such contrasts, and "expanded horizons" seemed to be faithful to the intent of Scripture. I said about halfway through the sermon:

> There is a difference between an expanded ego and an expanded horizon. The first is caught up with itself; it does not center on *other* great possibilities. The latter, although more difficult to discern, is infinitely more important to the self in the long run. An expanded horizon helps us to look beyond the sorrows and the shortcomings of the present to a hopeful future. It assists us to see things we would never see otherwise

about ourselves and the world. It enables us to do things we never considered possible, and we are changed into persons we never thought we could or would become. Faith is a way to describe expanded horizons.

I tried to say that Christian discipleship could be the response to "Follow me" as an "expanded horizon," full of growth and possibilities for the individual. On the other hand I had to apply the sermon to the annual meeting, which at first I found difficult. I began the sermon on Tuesday of the week, then after "living with the quotation" and doing some research on the text on Wednesday I personally typed my first draft, as I always do, which was in rough form, not "honed, polished, even rubbed." On Thursday I typed two more drafts, each time organizing my thoughts into more comprehensive shape and then including explicit references to the every member canvass, our fund raising efforts later in the year, our finances, the problems of the building and our program needs. I also used the "Gradual" hymn, sung before the Gospel, to help exemplify the meaning of discipleship. In our Hymnal it is number 437 and the first line is, "They cast their nets in Galilee, just off the hills of brown; such happy, simple fisherfolk, before the Lord came down."

On Friday my secretary typed the final draft, in large type (which is easier for me to read) since I am beginning to need bifocals, and then on Saturday I made a few changes in words and phrases.

Documentation of Sources

a. Gardner, John, "The World Was Not Designed for Our Personal Enjoyment," an excerpt from his book, *Morale* as printed in the *Stanford University Observer,* an alumni newspaper, p. 5, November 1978
b. St. Mark 1:14–20
c. Harvey, A. E., *The Companion to the New Testament*
d. The *1940 Hymnal,* Hymn 437

Number of Drafts and Time Taken

Four drafts, fifteen hours

Last Minute Changes of Thought

Towards the end of the week I became more bold about preaching to our church needs and injected a transition from private to corporate discipleship. I finally wrote:

> Program without deficit is a difficult tension to maintain and we may be the only parish doing such in the city. Yet our yearly challenge is to keep this church responding to the kingdom while refusing to allow it to become a small barren place where nets lie idle and our boat is full of dry rot . . . speaking of dry rot. . . .

This last sentence allowed me to move into church needs and when these were presented I was able to move back to personal discipleship again.

Possible Revision of Intention

My statement of intention remained the same: to speak to the personal and collective needs of the church about discipleship as a matter of expanded possibilities.

Hearing Group's Response

N.P. Began by saying that he found the subject of the sermon most appropriate for the occasion—tying in both the annual meeting and Venture in Mission program. He reacted well to your emphasis on the theme that being Christian calls for more than self-gratification. He does not believe that you present yourself as a confident preacher, of being at home in the pulpit, but your gifts are such that you shouldn't worry. He is theologically sound; no quarrel with what you say.

W.B. Liked your opposition of expanding ego to expanding horizons—he thought that a good box to put the sermon in. When you got to the part of your sermon which he said it shook him up—and got his full attention—because he couldn't see how you were going to get back to the main thrust of your sermon. He and others agreed that your discussion of concrete needs was effective and your ability to tie it in with the rest of the sermon was a virtuoso performance.

N.P.   Agreed that he came full circle.

S.B.   Thought this one of your best sermons, in fact. She was impressed with how you were able to appeal on theological, intellectual, and emotional levels. She felt that the point about the world not being made for our pleasure an intrusion (in part because she doesn't agree with it) but that otherwise it was an extremely effective sermon. He began with too loud a voice but later projected it to her.

J.K. (Jimmye Kimmey, the recorder)   "My own reaction to the sermon began with the singing of the Gradual hymn and, since you made mention of it in your sermon, I guess it is appropriate to say that that hymn is one I find so moving that I cannot sing it. That, combined with your discussion of calling, resonated with my continuing internal dialogue about my own call. When you began to discuss the financial needs of the parish my response was quite irrelevant—I felt uncomfortable because I was reminded of my own precarious financial condition."

The group feels uncertain that this is the sort of response you want and would be grateful for any guidance you can give it if you wish.

Sermon Number Two

MANY MESSENGERS

The Lord . . . sent persistently to them by his messengers, because he had compassion upon his people.—II Chronicles 36:14–23

At times all of us are God's messengers, although we may not be taken seriously and we may be wrong: at the same time all of us are often like the Israelites in our Old Testament lesson who do not recognize the mercy of God, become subject to evil, and then are eventually restored.

The hymn we have just sung this morning is one of my favorites. I would like it to be sung at my burial, but I wouldn't dare choose it because, in good conscience, I could never live up to its lyrics. Words such as "Once to every man and nation comes the moment to decide," are of special quality and actually form part of a poem, entitled "The Present Crisis," which was written in 1845 by James Russell Lowell, as a protest against our war with Mexico which he deplored as unjust aggression. His poem, it is believed, expressed his fear that annexation of the Southwest would increase the extent of slaveholding territory. From the original work of 90 lines, 16 were later chosen and finally entered our Hymnal in 1916. The sacred often derives from the secular.

The hymn's tune is also a favorite of mine, and not just because I am of Welsh descent, but because the melody's vigorous rhythm matches the strength and power of the words. The tune, called "Ton-y-Botel" is taken from a Welsh anthem, "Light in the Valley," and was written by Thomas John Williams, a Welshman if I ever knew one. Published in 1890 it was widely sung throughout Wales before publication, during which time the legend sprang up of its having been washed to shore off the coast of Wales, hence the name—John Cartwright reminds me—Ton-y-Botel, or quite simply, tune in a bottle.

So the hymn combines a robust tune, like many of the Welsh melodies in our Hymnal, with words of Christian protest. Although I do not recall that this hymn was sung in any service of social witness in the "Age of Protest," the 1960s, I have used it time and time again in churches when we approached moments of decision and of change, new occasions which "teach new duties," when "time makes ancient good uncouth," and when church and society at large must "upward still and onward, who would keep abreast of truth."

In the Old Testament lesson this morning it appears that the Hebrews had not kept abreast of truth nor of "new duties" because the author of Chronicles records that Israel had mocked the many messengers of God, had despised God's word and scoffed at the prophets. In terms of the world view or outlook of this writer, a judgment of history befell the Israelites. They were defeated, taken captive, and made slaves by the Babylonians. He called such devastation "the wrath of God," a phrase which makes me extremely uncomfortable, and yet he claimed that the prior warnings from many messengers had in fact revealed the compassion of God, but they were ignored. In a way, we are all like these Hebrews, at least I am. I know I have received "signals" from friends and loved ones which were meant for my welfare and which I did not heed; I have known moments when I felt estranged from God, or simply alone in an awful freedom without recourse to aid from any source; other times I have experienced a turning within me, a new growth and awareness, and then a sense of restoration.

Sometimes hymns, scripture, literature, poems have moved me to rethink my life or my direction, even though I did not always like what I read or what was said to me. James Russell Lowell may have been an unpopular messenger of truth, and if we borrow for a moment the mindset of our ancient, unnamed Biblical historian or chronicler, Lowell could well have been a spokesman for God's compassion, and his words may still cause many of us to stop and think. Yet he did not keep this country from warring with Mexico nor did he prevent the spread of slavery, and later the Civil War would be fought, "some great cause, God's new Messiah." Again the judgment of history would fall on us as it did on those ancient Jews and our land would also be put to the sword.

Do you believe that protest can be a sign of God's love, or are poets like Lowell just troublemakers who meddle in politics and who stand in the way of progress? I think there are times when we are called to be faithful troublemakers: it is the nature of the church to be concerned with the world, and when we take unpopular stands from conscience we may be unwitting, even unfit vehicles of God's mercy. The real trouble with most of us today is that we probably don't protest enough. Social injustice is never a sole concern for faddists but is an integral part of the Gospel for committed and informed Christians.

After all, as our hymn states, our faith was born on a scaffold, by the execution of an innocent man whom we call son of God and son of man, whose terribly wrong death revealed the ultimate expression of God's compassion for human suffering. Because of this cross, when we really think about it, things for us are completely different. It is as if we are, as Christian people, a mirror image of the world or we see some things upside down. No one in his right mind would follow with his life an executed peacemaker, or place values of this one's preaching above those of normal society, or consider seriously the vocation of a crucified one if that vocation were seen most clearly in the light of being unpopular but necessary messengers of God's compassion.

I must confess, however, that it is difficult to balance properly the roles of pastor and prophet, as it is difficult for any of us to square beliefs with actions, hypocrites that we are! Yet we too are called to speak from conscience, as ill informed as it may be, as fallible as we may be, as misguided as we may also be. No one person speaks the truth alone, even James Lowell, because inevitably wars are fought and then ended, and new occasions bring new peace, the Jews are released by an unexpected act of clemency by a foreign ruler, and civil wars, like Vietnam wars, do end. We can not tell if we speak the truth in the long run, but speak we must for the moment, in fear and trembling, in the "present crisis," as Lowell wrote. It is my conscience, for example, which tells me that any parish must be open to God's new spirit, to new people—not just because it is pragmatic to do so but because it is the nature of the Christian community not to be exclusive. I know that a parish cannot be solely concerned about itself but with those outside it, because we are all asked to be a Christ to our neighbors. I know that a parish must support ministries in areas where we alone would be completely ineffective, and not because it makes us feel good about ourselves but again because we are called to be so concerned. You have been asked to support Venture in Mission. Not because it will solve all the problems of society or by itself bring in the Kingdom, but because we are not sufficient to ourselves, we are part of a larger diocesan and greater Christian family which is badly hurting in places.

As a pastor I would not be worth my salt, as a man, if I always agreed with each of you. Everyone is his or her own person. There is much room in our Christian faith for not following the pack, for speaking your mind, and making yourself heard, because God does call us to be messengers of compassion in unique, individual, and many strange ways.

But I am too much like these Israelites of old, and I will not have this hymn sung at my burial. The words are beyond my reach even though they have impressed themselves on my spirit and have disturbed my conscience. I hope that they bother you also and stir you to the fact that all is not at ease in Zion, and we have much to do about ourselves, our parish, and society. In fact, offer in your worship today some injustice that you know of, pray about it, then follow your conscience as best you can remembering the last verse of Lowell's hymn:

> Though the cause of evil prosper,
> Yet 'tis truth alone is strong
> though her portion be the scaffold
> and upon the throne be wrong.
> Yet that scaffold sways the future
> and beyond the dim unknown
> standeth God within the shadow
> keeping watch above his own.

God does not ask that we be right, only that we be faithful.

Personal Record and Discussion of Sermon

Sources of Inspiration

The prime source of inspiration for this sermon was my favorite hymn, number 519 in the Episcopal Hymnal, "Once to Every Man and Nation." It stirred me to research the background of the hymn's melody, which is Ton-y-Botel, or Welsh for "tune in a bottle," and its lyrics, taken from poet James Russell Lowell's larger poem written in 1845 as a protest against our war with Mexico.

I have used the hymn time and time again where I believed parishes approached moments of decision and of change, new occasions which "teach new duties" when "time makes ancient good uncouth" and when church and society at large must "upward still and onward, who would keep abreast of the truth."

Choice of Method

The original intention was to preach that all Christians can be messengers of Christian ethical protest in society, through the use of this hymn.

Intention of Sermon

The method was deliberate from the beginning; to use a source other than Scripture as a base for my Sunday sermon. I have termed this method "cultural source."

Personal Record

The text is always important in my sermons, but I have preached more often from the New Testament than the Old for reasons which are simply of personal theological preference. In any case, I used Chronicles' story of Israel's mocking many messengers of God. The text was taken from II Chronicles 36:14–23 and was the Old Testament lesson of the day. It was narrowed to this line: "The Lord . . . sent persistently to them by his messengers because he had compassion on his people."

I exaggerated the text, especially the "wrath of God" which was the judgment of exile on the Hebrews for neglecting his messengers. I emphasized that God's compassion motivated sending messengers. All of us have received

> signals from friends and loved ones which were meant for my welfare and which I did not need. I have known moments when I felt estranged from God, or simply alone in an awful freedom without recourse.

I thought that to ask the listener to borrow a mindset from the author of Chronicles was fair, and that all of us are called to be "messengers of compassion," faithful troublemakers, even though no one of us has a complete glimpse of truth for our times.

Then I hit upon the idea that we speak the truth only for the "present crisis," as Lowell said in his hymn, and so prophecy is limited. I also wanted to speak about balancing "prophet with pastor" and about parishes, in general, not being exclusive, but inclusive, and compassionate. I must confess that I wrote the first draft of the sermon in one day in the country as I joined my wife while she was still vacationing from teaching school. I returned to the city and typed two drafts on Saturday, and "played with it" some more before I preached on Sunday. Towards the end of the week I became more personal, more "Ernest Hunt" speaking, than the words of James Russell Lowell.

Documentation of Sources
a. II Chronicles 36:14–28
b. *Interpreter's Bible*, Volume 3
c. *Hymnal 1940*, Hymn 519
d. *Hymnal Companion*, page 159

Number of Drafts and Time Taken
Three drafts, thirteen hours

Last Minute Changes of Thought
At the last minute I became bolder concerning a personal stance between prophet and pastor, and finally came up with this paragraph, near the end of the sermon, after some thoughtful soul searching:

> As pastor I would not be worth my salt, as a man, if I always agreed with each of you. Everyone is his or her own person. There is much room in our Christian faith for not following the pack, for speaking your mind, and making yourself heard, because God does call us to be messengers of compassion in unique, individual, and strange ways.

Possible Revision of Intention
I did not change the purpose of this sermon. As it was conceived so was it given birth.

Hearing Group's Response
J.N.   Loved the sermon—especially the beginning with the historical material, the use of the hymn, etc. But for a time after the opening her mind wandered a bit. She is not sure whether it is because you were not being as forceful and she resisted being shaken up.

N.P. Felt you are more relaxed and comfortable in this sermon than any others—that you are on your way to becoming a master! Was moved by this sermon—it came across as something you felt you *had* to say. As always he responded to your sincerity.

J.N. Said she came back to the sermon after her period of mind-wandering and, trying to understand why she had drifted away for a time, concluded it might have been caused by her *sense* that asking for money—and blessing it—is difficult for you.

J.N. and N.P. Agreed that your stress on the need to move ahead and not to stay in a rut, to want to change— was excellent. They thought some of that emphasis may have come from the vestry meeting.

N.P. Thinks you are getting better and better each time, probably because you are preaching so often—which, as you know, he thinks you should do.

J.K. "My response was different from that to any of the other sermons in that, unlike Janet, I stayed *with* this one in a particularly intimate way. In the others, I have at some point or points been led to think my own thoughts about something you said but this one was—it's hard to express—almost like listening to music which just kept pulling me along. There was a breadth and largeness to the development; there seemed to be time for everything to be said."

As we all agreed, it was a great experience.

Sermon Number Three

DON QUIXOTE OF THE JORDAN

John the Baptist preached a message about a coming Savior, which did prove to be true, and thus we modern Christians who yearn for justice, peace, and for goodness can hold to our ideals in the midst of personal and social disillusionment. Advent challenges us to risk more of ourselves.

John the Baptist was certainly no idealized religious figure, no Billy Graham. Rather he appears as a puzzling, paradoxical hermit, wearing clothes of camel hair, a rough leather belt, who ate wild locusts and lived off of wild honey. He was an ascetic, and in fulfillment of the Old Testament came from a wilderness similar to that which Jesus would enter after his baptism. John said, "The Kingdom of Heaven is at hand," which is to say, "God's rule is coming, that longed for state of affairs when men and women willingly and spontaneously respond to the ideal life in God."

Another paradoxical ascetic in literature, created by the sensitive Spanish writer, Miguel de Cervantes Saavedra, was Don Quixote de La Mancha. He and his companion, Sancho Panza, the idealistic knight and his greedy squire, the one on his lean nag Rozinante (whom he thought as regal as Alexander's Bucephalus) tilts at windmills, while the other astride his little burro, dreams of gold. They make us laugh, unlike the Baptist, even as they win only beatings and torments from an indifferent, uncomprehending, and cruel world. Don Quixote is a knight-errant, traversing the world, armed and mounted, in quest of chivalrous adventures and serving the undeserving but idealized maid "Dulcinea"; but he fights only imaginary enemies. As an unwitting idealist, Don Quixote's journeys only lead to a gradual disillusionment which slowly eats away his faith in himself and in humanity. The inability of human beings to alter or shape everyday events which befall them leads us to see ourselves in the prison of a fixed destiny. When despair destroys Quixote's faith, and his will to act, as in Hamlet, apathy sets in. "The very basis of values, which give meaning and direction to action, when destroyed, leave us only with death." Don Quixote is a classical figure and is insane. He distorts the true world—a tragic hero who believes that he can shape reality in the image of his chosen ideal. John's insanity, on the other hand, is in line with Biblical expectation. He too attempts to reshape the world, but soon realizes his limitations. Only the ideal itself, not our wilful expression of it, only Christ, not some Dulcinea we put on a pedestal of beauty, truth, and goodness, can truly transform the world.

Perhaps the reason I thought of Quixote when musing about John the Baptist is because the prophet is too difficult to understand or take seriously in today's world. He confronts everyone—"You brood of vipers"—and demands that everyone repent. John would understand nothing of politics, of the art of the possible, nor would he be able to maneuver in the ecclesiastical circles of his day to achieve the "highest good." His was an absolutist world of black and white, right and wrong. We are fortunate indeed that he did finally realize his limitations, that he preached no Dulcinea but a real savior. Consequently he is enshrined in the church as that uncompromising forerunner—a rogue of a prophet who went too far in his condemnation of the world and finally knew it. He was for certain no man of the world; he did not accept the Herods and Salomes of his time who still prevail. He makes no accommodation and thus his head is cut off. He who will not compromise is doomed, and if it were not for Jesus Christ, he would have been as much a failure as Don Quixote.

Yet both he and Cervantes' hero witness to an idealism this world needs in order to survive. If I did not have personal ideals, and were not somewhat of an idealist myself, I would not be addressing you today in this pulpit, nor would I have supported Prayer Book revision, central altars, the ordination of women, or expect Epiphany to raise this year $150,000 in pledges. To me these are all proper responses to the coming Kingdom, to a higher view of humanity and the church in relation to God. I ran across a leaflet from a former parish the other day which indicated I was using the "new Liturgy," as it was called, in 1969, a little like Don Quixote, hoping for the best. I suppose this is why Picasso's portrayal of Quixote hangs in my office.

Advent reminds us that God's Kingdom is always coming. We may tend to be a nation of pragmatists, but even those who deal with data only, who insist on the "concrete" and verifiable evidence for hope, need to be informed from some higher, outside reference. We resist idealism because of disillusionment, as Quixote's culture resisted him. Everything today is immediate "contact," the "here and now," and anything abstract confuses us. But idealism is only wrong when it is disassociated from a continuing faith, or when we can't understand despair, but John the Baptist always makes us try again, for we need another Kingdom to judge this one. We need heaven to live on earth. Albert Camus wrote: "If the words justice, goodness, and beauty have no meaning, then men can tear one another to pieces."

There was a tragedy in our parish this week. At the 9:15 homily of last Sunday Jayne Nikolic mentioned a Russian immigrant who was employed in our Every Monday Rummage Sale and sponsored in this country by the International Rescue Committee. He loved working with us—it was a second home, but he knew very little English. On Tuesday he stopped by the parish to meet Jayne about another job, but was an hour late and missed her. We tried to explain to him what had happened, and he brought out three books from his old valise, which he tightly clutched, as well as his glasses to see with, and together we used his dictionaries to help explain that he would have to wait until Friday to talk to her again. He lived in Far Rockaway in some small room to which he would have to return. I gave him a cup of coffee and he eventually left. I had just begun to know him, even if the only Russian word I could speak was "nyet."

On Thursday morning as I arrived at church I was asked to call Jayne who informed me that she had been called by the emergency room of St. John's Episcopal Hospital in Rockaway at 5:30 in the morning. Someone said that Mikhail was unconscious, and information was needed about him. Her name and number were found on his person, probably the note I had given him. Later in the morning we discovered that he had been ruthlessly assaulted, shot, and left for dead by no imaginary enemies. He had come to the land of freedom from oppression only to be gunned down on our streets.

We may tear ourselves to pieces unless we have ideals, unless enough people believe in that abstract higher Kingdom of

Heaven, and feel enough spiritual pressure from it to risk being Don Quixotes and John the Baptists. We need more idealists today to show us the way. I feel terrible about Mikhail, but this church is not going to stop helping people. I hope we have just begun.

When disillusionment occurs, and it will, we should look for a windmill to fight! Get on your Rozinante, battle your times, eat wild locusts or wild honey if need be, but look for the coming of Christ who alone fulfills the ideal and who does not disappoint us.

If it takes insanity to be faithful, then by all means be a knight-errant, a fool for Christ. It's about time more of us were.

Personal Record and Discussion of Sermon

Sources of Inspiration

It is sometimes difficult to understand the humanity of Biblical men and women. John the Baptist, for example, was an uncompromising prophet who confronted the world. He made no accommodation to its imperfections. "He who will not compromise is doomed." Is not politics the art of the possible? John was no politician.

I thought of Cervantes' *Don Quixote* when approaching my sermon in the second Sunday of Advent. He, too, was crazy, idealistic, difficult-to-understand—and yet a hero of mine for years. Hispanic-American studies and religion was the subject of my M.A. at Stanford University, and I have been attracted to some of the literature, and philosophy of both the New and Old World Spanish cultures since youth. My grandmother on my father's side was of the Porfirio Diaz family and born in Mexico. Spanish was my second language in schools in my home state of California. I've identified personally with Don Quixote many times in my life as a pastor, particularly as I encountered paradoxical situations. For this sermon I reopened my old copy of *Don Quixote,* and as I skimmed the pages I began to draw a parallel between him and John the Baptist.

Idealists may "have their heads in the clouds," but without

an idealistic outlook, or one which transcends the world, we would not be able to function as Christians when confronted by tragedy.

Another source of inspiration was a recent tragic shooting of a refugee who had been helped by our church. The story of Mikhail's difficulties was also very much on my mind.

Choice of Method

"Cultural sources" was the method I chose, mainly because the preparation of this sermon was initiated by rereading *Don Quixote*.

Intention of Sermon

My intention was to help the listener to understand John the Baptist better by referring to *Don Quixote*.

Personal Record

On Monday afternoon I looked at the coming Sunday's text (the second Sunday in Advent) and after reading two commentaries, I took *Don Quixote* off the shelf and home with me. That night I quickly read the book again, regaining a picture of this "unwitting idealist," whose journeys only led to disillusionment. The introduction to Cervantes' work by Lester G. Crocher was of such ethical and philosophical depth that I began to see John the Baptist as a Biblical Quixote, also as an uncompromising idealist. He did not seek a "Dulcinea," however, "but a real Savior." I played with this contrast and then on Wednesday (after being too busy to write on Tuesday) I approached my 30-year-old Underwood upright and started clacking keys. "Advent challenges us to risk more of ourselves," like John the Baptist. How? By being an idealist, by being witnesses for the Kingdom of God, that "ideal life of God." I contrasted Quixote and the Baptist, calling John "a rogue of a prophet who went too far in the condemnation of the world and finally knew it." Yet, I wrote, we need idealism to survive as Christians.

Then I thought personally about idealism. "If I did not have personal ideals, and were not somewhat of an idealist myself, I would not be addressing you today in the pulpit, nor would I have supported Prayer Book renewal, central altars, or ordination of women." I interjected these three Episcopalian issues which have caused controversy because I wanted to show that it was my faith, not some momentary faddism, which motivated my own stands in the past. This is not to say that new forms of worship are always right, or that central altars will bring in the Kingdom, or that the ordination of women to the priesthood does not have to stand the test of time and of the Spirit to be accepted by the universal church. I can only speak for myself. To be a visionary means to risk; but Jesus risked all, and so did the Baptist. I also recalled using the "new liturgy" of the Episcopal Church in 1969, in Creve Coeur, and said, "I suppose this is why Picasso's portrayal of Quixote hangs in my office." I stopped at this point and went to another task.

I returned later to the Underwood, with a half-written page waiting patiently for completion. It's difficult to have inspiration on demand each week, and I sympathize with true writers. Madeleine L'Engle has said that writing is 90% discipline, and about half will be thrown away. I always have the feeling that each sermon I write should be thrown away! But I preach each anyway.

When I arrived at my office on Thursday morning the phone rang. Jayne Nikolic, Chairman of our Every Monday Rummage Sale (don't be confused, this is a weekly community ministry which employs alcoholic outpatients of East Harlem Hospital and newly arrived refugees of all countries), told me that our man from Russia had been shot in the head. I remembered that on Tuesday, the day I didn't write, that I had seen him. I was upset, as she was. I had just gotten to know him (he said in broken English that working in the church, although he was not a Christian, was the only happy time in his week). This tested my idealism, and I turned to Camus. What did he say about ideals? I read some notes on his *Lyrical and Critical Essays* which I painstakingly made in Creve Coeur in 1968, and applied them to my own understanding of the tragedy which had just occurred. He wrote: "If the words justice, goodness, and beauty have no meaning, then men can tear one another to pieces." More than ever I concluded, "We need heaven to live on earth."

Then I directed my attention to the congregation. In my writing I charged them, "We need to feel enough spiritual pressure" from (the abstract higher Kingdom of God) to risk being Don Quixotes and John the Baptists. I completed four pages on Thursday and went home.

Friday morning I reread what I had written and typed another draft and gave it to my secretary for final typing.

Documentation of Sources

a. Lester G. Crocher, editor, *Don Quixote de La Mancha,* Miguel de Cervantes Saavedra, Washington Square Press, New York, 1969

b. Philip Thody, editor, *Lyrical and Critical Essays,* Albert Camus, Knopf, New York, 1968

c. A. E. Harvey, *Companion to the New Testament*

d. *Interpreter's Bible,* Vol. 8

e. R. H. Fuller, *Luke's Witness to Jesus Christ,* Association Press, New York, 1958

f. Gospel of St. Luke 3:1–6

Number of Drafts and Time Taken

Five drafts, twenty hours

Last Minute Changes of Thought

The introduction into the sermon of my experience with a Russian refugee certainly added to my contrast of Don Quixote and of the Baptist. In fact, it changed the drift of my sermon and reinforced my growing conviction, "We need heaven to live on earth" to understand tragedy.

Possible Revision of Intention

I did revise my intention. The simple contrast for the sake of understanding now became secondary to the tragedy of our refugee. Now I wanted the listener to become an idealist. "When disillusionment occurs, and it will, we should look for a windmill to fight!" I asked for more "fools for Christ."

5

Pastoral
Situation Method

In this methodology, which begins at the inception of thinking and writing, preparation has to do with envisioning a recipient of the sermon as one whose problem in some way is addressed by the underlying text. As I have said, this is a way suggested by Harry Emerson Fosdick, one-time pastor and preacher of Riverside Church in New York City. Fosdick was a powerful advocate of the disenfranchised in society and of those who suffer from injustice. He urged that we begin with a "life issue," a genuine problem in the community or city so that our hearers will become involved in the pastoral dimensions of their own ability to minister. Or we can begin from a personal issue which confronts us such as in the case with the sermon, "The Suffering of My Father." Therefore the direction in this method is from "pastoral situation" through imagination, or the internalizing, conflict process already discussed, to "text" with possible use of "cultural sources" to follow.

Since the methods have already been introduced and discussed elsewhere and their effect on my congregation analyzed in a later chapter, a word should be said again about the theology of preaching to a pastoral situation before the sermons are read. As I stated earlier, I believe that God reveals himself in the suffering and needs of people, and not in spite of them. The church witnesses to God's mercy and compassion for all people. Pastoral needs are addressed because the church is called to transform society, as H. R. Niebuhr advocated in his book, *Christ and Culture.* We address social wrongs; it is the challenge of the preacher to address the ills of society as a spokesman for the church, and he or she may at times stand in judgment on social sin, or at least bring a perspective to society which it would not have without some reference to ultimacy. Therefore, this method presumes a *theology of transformation of the world,* where the ideal is applied to the real.

Obviously, I believe that we can change the conditions which imprison some individuals, whether afflicted by social wrongs or by physical or mental disease. Otherwise, I would have no integrity of approach. The world is not an end in itself, but needs light from another source, and that source is the Kingdom of God as Jesus taught it. Whenever we witness glimpses of justice, mercy, compassion, we see the Kingdom break through into our life. As preachers we aim to help our listeners become aware of the possibilities of grace, of the numerous breakthroughs they will witness when they care enough and when they commit themselves to alleviating human need. Although I am a tamed cynic, as Reinhold Niebuhr once called himself, I am also an optimist of sorts. If we can't change human nature or the structures of society, or at least think that we can have an impact on them, then we become complete cynics. We are only optimists because of the Gospel, not because we are primarily believers in social reform.

I can address a pastoral situation precisely because God has addressed my own sin in the healing and reconciliation of his Son; a preacher's confidence is not in himself, but in his "Gospel" calling.

Sermon Number One

LONELINESS

Prayer, often alone by oneself, can help our loneliness and enable us to find purpose. One of the loneliest places in the world is a hospital, and perhaps one of the loneliest hospitals in the world is Memorial nearby. The aloneness of a terminally ill patient is often magnified by the comparison of his or her incapacity to that of the impersonal activity of the healthy who come and go through hospital doors and hallways each day for pay. JoAnn Kelly Smith in a book called *Free-Fall* describes being terminally ill and experiencing a personal aloneness more radical than the normal loneliness we feel. She writes:

> As my illness progresses, my sense of isolation increases. Aloneness is one of the worst of all human experiences. And I have it day after day. Jesus could not overcome that, and I find some understanding that if he couldn't why should I think I can span its abyss.

In St. Mark's Gospel Jesus has just spent the whole day in Capernaum healing sick people and he is spiritually and physically exhausted. He is also concerned lest his healing be misconstrued as an act which brings him praise instead of a way which helps people understand his purpose. And so early next morning he leaves his disciples and goes away to a lonely spot and remains there in prayer. He chooses solitude, but not without purpose. It was a kind of voluntary "free-fall," a way of letting go from the demands of individuals and the crowds, like a good doctor who has been hours in surgery and is drained, exhausted, and needs to rest and recuperate so that he can continue to heal. In a way, Jesus did the same thing, even while some who were ill probably hoped for his attention. Simon and his companions searched him out, found him, and said, "They are all looking for you," but he said, "Let us move on. . . . I have come to proclaim my message . . . that is what I came out to do." I wonder how many JoAnn Kelly Smiths he left behind in Capernaum. Of course, St. Mark's narrative about the Kingdom of God, and these particular healing incidents are not written as ends in themselves, but as signs of who this one is, the lonely Messiah from Nazareth.

What he did when he was alone in prayer we can only imagine. He may have uttered words aloud or meditated silently; he may have recited the Torah or lines from Isaiah, he may have seized his silent opportunity as a moment for creative anguish, a time to cry out for insight, for forgiveness, and for help. Perhaps he simply needed to overcome that strange, almost eery loneliness one feels in the midst of crowds. New Yorkers often experience a diminished sense of self-worth when pressed on city streets by nameless people who do not seem to care about them as persons.

Jesus was a lonely person, but he consistently rediscovered his purpose—his worth—through prayer by himself. He could almost be called a loner because he did not seem to need groups of people for personal support. Yet he was by no means anti-social, because he was constantly engaged with people—their needs, their hopes, their fears. But he left his family and he traveled incessantly, spending most of his time with crowds and groups of enemies, on the one hand, or individuals in need of help and a few close friends on the other. While his whole life was an offering of himself he rejected any form of praise. Former Secretary General of the United Nations, Dag Hammarskjold, once wrote:

> Praise nauseates you—but woe betide him who does not recognize your worth.

Some recognized who Jesus was, but for him to receive their praise would mean that outside forces sustained a person instead of those within, and Jesus, the lonely Messiah, knew that inner worth came from prayer alone. Consequently, Jesus drew to himself lonely people, those who had been shunned by others, Mary Magdalene, Matthew the tax gatherer, a variety of fishermen, and even a few misguided zealots. He still draws us to himself today because he is our atonement, our at-one-ment with God, and he is so through us, this church, this parish, which is needed today by so many people in the loneliest city

of them all. What we discover here is that aloneness is part of
the universal human condition; we do not deny it. There are
times we need to be alone and times we can't stand to be alone;
there are moments when we feel intense loneliness and other
occasions when we do not, but our hope, and our faith is reinforced by the fact that all of this was shared by the Son of God,
by the same one who made us one with God through dying on
the cross.

When Jesus prayed alone on that day in Capernaum perhaps
he also prayed for strength to face his death, because he knew
what was ultimately ahead of him, like JoAnn Kelly Smith. She
writes:

> Someone said the way we handle the many separations which
> come in our life's experiences will determine how we face the
> biggest one—death . . . and I have always found all separation
> hard.

She describes the difference between aloneness and loneliness:

> Being all alone . . . (is) because no one else can be with you no
> matter how much you want him or how much he wants to be
> with you. It is the feeling of free fall. You must do it alone. But
> there is also loneliness in separation.

> Loneliness is a sense of emptiness—caught without a way out.

> Loneliness is being abandoned.

> Loneliness is without company.

While there is the aloneness of a patient in Memorial Hospital on York Avenue, there is also a painful loneliness of young
people at Maxwell's Plum on First Avenue, an emptiness which
surfaces in quick encounters, a reaching out for another to take
away the pain of life lived alone, to make one seem almost im-
mortal, to find some self-worth. There is the loneliness of the
single or married person who feels abandoned in midlife when
jobs change, family ties are severed, cultural expectations of
personhood change, and children leave. There is also that terrible loneliness of the elderly person who needs support while
struggling to remain independent and physically capable.

And yet our Lord chose to be alone and sought the quiet of a mountain or a wilderness or a place away from his followers to find himself and his destiny; so being alone can be sanctified.

The church exists for people to rediscover a purpose, not through random encounters but meaningful relationships, not just through some quick word of praise, but sustaining support, not just by forgetting what is ahead for us all, but dealing with it through faith.

All of us are in a kind of "free fall" just like JoAnn Kelly Smith, and so our experience is the same as that of the lonely Messiah of Nazareth. Thank God he is a savior who shared our frailty and who shows us that being alone can be a source of strength as being a part of his body, the church, can help us transform loneliness. Dag Hammarskjold knew how important it was to find direction through prayer in his own lonely life; he said: "Pray that your loneliness may spur you into finding something to live for, great enough to die for . . . " and so the same was true for the man from Nazareth, who took the time to pray in order to get moving again, and it can be the same for each of us.

Personal Record and Discussion of Sermon

Sources of Inspiration

The source of inspiration for this sermon was the plight of the church sexton's wife, who, at the time, was diagnosed as having cancer of the mouth. She was poor and she was in pain. Before my arrival as rector, the vestry had argued about medical coverage for the sexton, but had not decided to proceed because of the proposer's resignation. Later, when I discovered the sexton had no medical insurance (he resisted talking about it because he is an independent soul), I was able to obtain it for him but not for his wife. Later, I was able to assist her entry into Memorial Hospital in New York City, even though she had no insurance. All her life she had been a recluse and no one in the parish knew her; then all of a sudden she was faced with 1) hospital, 2) surgery, 3) chemotherapy. The day of her admittance I helped carry her down five flights of stairs at her walk-up apartment, negotiated with Memorial's admitting office, and later, after she was in her hospital room, morally supported her husband as best I could.

The sexton has had a real ministry, which all people of our church recognize. Finally, in six months, the sexton's wife's ordeal was over. When she died, however, she left about $40,000 in outstanding medical bills, but we were influential in persuading the hospital to "forgive" the sexton's debts.

As I began this sermon, I wanted to address the loneliness of suffering, which turned out to be my worst struggle to date. It should be understood that Epiphany's ministry concerns a witness to lonely people, singles, the elderly, the divorced, those about to marry or be remarried after divorce, and those who are in hospitals.

Choice of Method

I chose "pastoral situation" as my source and moved from it to cultural sources, conflict, and text.

Intention of Sermon

My intention was to speak to loneliness and to offer hope through prayer, the examples of brave people who suffer, and our Lord's own life.

Personal Record

One often encounters indifference to pain in hospitals. For the sick a hospital can be impersonal, antiseptic, and nonemotional. Consequently, it seems to me that one task of a preacher is to help his listeners become more empathetic to the needs of those who are ill. My mind "leap-frogged" from a concrete situation of the sexton's plight (which I could not mention from the pulpit) to general hospital experiences. Then I looked to my bookshelves for a book I remembered, called *Free-Fall*, by JoAnn Kelly Smith, who described the stages of her own dying from cancer. I had also been reading Dag Hammarskjold's book *Markings* because I remembered he was a lonely man. The text, "He went to a lonely spot and remained there in prayer" meant to me that loneliness can also be transformed. I hit upon the idea of comparing the free-fall of a terminal patient to the "free-fall" of Jesus as he approached his own end. I portrayed Jesus as I thought I caught a glimpse of him in this text, wanting to be alone, wanting to pray, to find himself in order to *move on* again.

I moved toward a conclusion as I finally wrote my thoughts down on paper, then went through a first draft on Wednesday.

> The church exists for people to rediscover a purpose, not through random encounters, but meaningful relationships; not just some grand word of prose, but sustaining support; not just by forgetting what is ahead for us all, but dealing with it through faith.

When I approached my third draft and again handed my four pages to be typed by my secretary, I remembered Hammarskjold's phrase, "Pray that your loneliness may spur you into finding something to live for, great enough to die for," and then went back to Jesus for the example of loneliness used to "get moving again."

Documentation of Sources
a. JoAnn Kelly Smith, *Free-Fall*
b. Dag Hammarskjold, *Markings*
c. St. Mark 1:29–39
d. A. E. Harvey, *The Companion to the New Testament*
e. *The Interpreter's Bible,* Vol. 7

Number of Drafts and Time Taken
Three drafts, thirteen hours

Last Minute Changes of Thought
I did not have any sudden last minute changes of thought, but I do remember that this was a tense sermon, one which made me become caught up in its meaning. I did include, "I wonder how many JoAnn Kelly Smiths he (Jesus) left behind at Capernaum" because my own conflict about not helping as many people as possible needed to be expressed, or at least I thought so, and so I did.

Possible Revision of Intention

My final result was pretty much the same as my original intention except I centered more and more at the end on Smith and Hammarskjold as sources for dealing with loneliness. I did not revise my purpose.

Hearing Group's Response

N.P.   "The purpose of the sermon, I believe, was to be comforting (in the Latin sense) and it was well-conceived and well-executed." Connection between prayer and loneliness was good—but would have liked more on the *receiving* end of prayer. What from prayer is strengthening?

W.B.   Agreed with Pusey—including feeling that the part on prayer was almost an incomplete thought.

J.N.   Picked up on that remark saying, maybe we need to hear how to be strong. Parenthetical remarks that so many examples (the book, D. H., Jesus, hospital, Maxwell's Plum) detracted from main point.

N.P.   Point of the sermon might have been *"we are not alone."* But that didn't come through.

S.B.   Thought it a fine sermon (as did the whole group), especially liked its *being focused*.

J.N.   Was very taken, as were SB and others, with the emphasis on prayer—but wanted more on how to pray. To which NP added—and how to be receptive.

S.B.   Disturbed by phrase which she understood to say that one's inherent worth is derived by prayer—i.e., by how much one prays—but she was very positive about the sermon saying she liked the sense she had that it came very much from you, i.e., from the heart.

N.P.   Agreed, saying Ernie never says anything that isn't sincere and he is getting more confident and that it shows—*the trumpet is getting more certain*—great leadership potential.

J.N. Liked it because it was clear that prayer is important to you.

J.K. Everyone agreed that your manner of delivery was excellent—much more at ease—speaking with authority. JN remarked that she had forgotten today was an evaluation day so reacted unselfconsciously—she felt comfortable because of your confidence.

"The group reacted more to the prayer aspect of the sermon, but I was caught more by the theme of *aloneness*. The pictures of Jesus going apart, to be alone to pray, have been important to me. I suppose because it has always been important to me to be alone to regenerate. The way you dealt with aloneness in the sermon was, as NP said, comforting—in the Latin sense."

Sermon Number Two

THE SUFFERING OF MY FATHER

Involvement with people in need means that we will feel their suffering, encounter moral conflicts, and make mistakes in judgment. Yet I know that the process of becoming more vulnerable to others can lead us to the discovery that life is a gift for which we should give thanks.

The Epistle to the Romans is really a testament to St. Paul's personal faith. This particular text refers to Paul's own conflicts about himself in relation to God and contains words which more or less began my "conversion" process in college: "For I do not what I want, but I do the very thing I hate . . . who will deliver me from this body of death?" Of course, Paul discourses here about the meaning of evil; he objectifies it as a power in a person and assumes that we are subject to outside forces which subjugate and master us. How does one free himself from sin? The old Jewish self in Paul would have said, "Obey the law," but his new Christian self says, "When liberated to serve others in righteousness we are not subject to sin but to

Christ, as Lord." But I identified not so much with his answer *but with his struggle,* with his perception that there is an irrational streak in each of us and that in life we may witness sufferings which seem unfair and unjust. At least, his words over the years have stood out in my mind and I still refer to them in difficult situations.

As a nonchurchgoer at the time, who decided to take elective courses in religious studies, I explored an area of knowledge which was interesting but unfamiliar. I was not affected, however, by the reality in religion, until St. Paul's words, discussed in a class taught by a dour Scottish Presbyterian divine, touched me personally. If this places me in the same theological stream as Wesley, Luther, and Augustine—all deeply influenced by Paul's conflicts—then so be it. I am willing to be a spiritual descendant of the apostle. We are justified by revealing our needs to God and not by denying our humanity.

Paul's own conflicts made him seem as human as I was. Therefore the Christianity he espoused became attractive to me, and I attended church through friends and was baptized.

Now I realize years later that we are all like Paul. We never cease to be pilgrims on an ultimate journey, often beset and confused by life's labyrinths and mazes, detours, and wrong paths, sudden reversals, and drawnout retreats. Even heaven is an uncharted map for us, whose new experience of ourselves and of God is best left obscured by mystery and assumed by faith.

There is a great difference, however, between studying the life and work of religious leaders and then experiencing religion as a new outlook on the world, a perspective from which to know oneself and ultimate things, a far-seeing way to understand human suffering and human love.

To be an observer, however, is not to become involved, to be a student of a subject is not necessarily to be a participant in its meaning, although this may be more true of religion than of science.

While we encourage the study of religion, we know the impact of religious faith occurs when we are lifted out of ourselves for a short time to discover that we are not so guilty as we thought, that we are not ultimately forsaken, and that there is a personal dimension to the universe which is not remote but becomes one with us in suffering and redemption.

The difference between observing and participating is especially acute among those who are ill. We may see the sickness of another but until we are drawn into the experience of the disability of that person, we are spectators, not participants. For example, my father had a near fatal stroke five and a half years ago, and he has been hospitalized ever since. Because he has had a strong heart he has lived through the many bouts of pneumonia, virus infections, and other short-lived physical problems which occur to stroke victims. My father has been in a kind of prison, serving some unknown and unreasonable sentence, frustrated because he is unable to speak, unable to walk, barely able to move, unable to swallow, and yet still capable of expression. Recently a sudden reversal of his general condition occurred which has produced slow heart failure, ever so slow, each breath a last gasp, and yet day after day his heart keeps pumping and the peace of death will not come. He can still be nourished, antibiotics can still control infection, and oxygen can yet assist his breathing. The good doctor says, "I am merely doing my job" in supplying simple life supports. Still the conscious gasping continues and will only terminate when the heart, as a natural organ, stops at last. Yet it beats on like a clock, marking all our time. My father reflexively looks at his watch on his good left hand and life continues.

My stepmother asked me a question when I visited him last week, "Why has God been mean to me?" We stayed up late one night talking about God's will, that he does not cause suffering but shares it, that prayer is accepting what is, that God has become involved in us through the cross and yet he leaves us subject in freedom to the same forces which wounded Jesus. Is there an answer? Not an absolute one, at least. God has proven that he is not "mean" by dying our death, by entering into human travail and allowing us to see his weakness, his vulnerability, his love—because love is sharing, and is participating; it is being involved, even when it is unequitably hell.

Christians are always seekers of the reason why; we keep

probing, even after we are "converted," we keep searching for answers, because we, too, are still imprisoned in flesh and blood. "Wretched man that I am, who will deliver me from this body of death?" I don't know if my father has asked that question of himself, but I have asked it for him. Who will deliver us? When I was in California last week I recalled the words of Paul, which led me to the church and to my vocation: "For I know that nothing good dwells within me." And then I remember Paul's resolution of the human conflict by saying finally, "Thanks be to God through Jesus Christ our Lord."

To say thanks after moral conflict and involvement in suffering is not courageous nor is it absurd, it is all that is left, it is the last word, the only alternative to bitterness and to remorse, it is the final conclusion for being given the gift of life in the first place, as incomplete as it may be for some. I believe more than ever that our present conflicts and sufferings are preludes to a nobler life to come, not just here, as important as it is to be fully involved in the redemption of the world, but beyond time, space, and history. I think the older I am the more I believe in Eternal Life, in that other dimension to this frail existence that our Lord taught and which is meant to transform human societies. No pastor could be who he or she is without the Kingdom, for Heaven is total involvement because it is where love is fully experienced. If we are now subject to Christ, then only God's love can become our ultimate guide.

The response now, it seems to me, is pretty simple, it is still in Paul's words, "Thanks be," even when we do not know why, even when we do not have the answers. Faith may not be a discovery of reasons, but it begins with struggle to be thankful in the face of suffering, to be thankful for the involvement of God himself in our lives through Christ.

Personal Record and Discussion of Sermon

Sources of Inspiration

The inspiration for this sermon was the result of my father's terminal illness, my trip to California to see him, and my ministry to my stepmother there. My Dad had a nearly fatal stroke in 1974. He lost his ability to speak, swallow, was incontinent, and was completely paralyzed on one side. He was fed through a tube in his stomach for most of those years, and spent his days in a "rehabilitation center" near the Bay Area of California. He was cared for faithfully by my devoutly Roman Catholic stepmother who almost kept a vigil by his side. He did relearn, or remember in some way, to recognize and communicate to people through facial expressions and gestures with his good left hand. He could watch television for a short time and he did learn to eat again until bouts with pneumonia, and his relatively immobile condition, began to weaken his heart. He had constant choking spasms because of accumulation of fluid in his lungs and his inability to swallow. The end of his struggle was near, and my stepmother asked me to come to her aid, which I did for a week's visit in the middle of Lent.

While in the rehabilitation center during the week, and after fighting a virus myself, I began, almost as an escape for a short time from his bedside, to write about his illness, to describe it; and so my sermon was conceived.

Choice of Method

The method was an obvious outgrowth of the "pastoral situation." I needed to address this condition and all people who suffer from irreversible illness.

Intention of Sermon

My intention at first was to speak to the condition of suffering through my own personal faith and to present the case of my father as an example.

Personal Record

There were three developments in my thought for this sermon while I was in California: the first, as I mentioned, grew out of my own confrontation with my father's anguished physical state. The second was that my return to California also allowed me to visit my son at Stanford University, my own alma mater, and to share experiences on campus with him. My return to Stanford was most pleasant, except that I began to remember—probably because of my father—my own process of conversion to Christianity. The text, which I usually take from the Gospel, I chose instead from the Epistle because it contained Paul's words from Romans:

> For I do not do what I want, but I do the very thing I hate. Who will deliver me from this body of death?

It was precisely those words which stand out in my mind as the nucleus of my conversion, not that it was a sudden event. It was more of a movement away from diffident atheism to acceptance of deity and of the church, a process fed by friends, and especially by one person. That movement was nurtured by the need to be intellectually honest as I approached the citadel of religion, with prejudice and hostility against it which was my gift from my family since birth. It was Paul's own anguish concerning moral conflict which seemed to be of comfort *again* to me as I came to my father after many years of separation. As I wrote, I thought of the Pauline phrase, the "old man" versus the "new man," and how I had changed. I also researched Paul's words by using Nygren's *Commentary on Romans* as well as other commentaries, and presented the best representation of their meaning as I could for this sermon. "But I identified not so much with his answer," I wrote, "but with his struggle." I developed the theme of conversion plus sanctification, continued growth leading to heaven, "a journey without maps," as Melville wrote.

> I am willing to be a spiritual descendant of the apostle. We are justified by revealing our needs to God and not by denying our humanity. Paul's own conflicts made him seem as human as I was. Therefore the Christianity he espoused became attractive to me, and I attended church through friends and was baptized.

The third development was my effort to address my stepmother's questions, which became for me universal ones, shared by me and certainly by the congregation I would address when I returned to New York City.

After describing my father's life as a "prison," and he "serving some unknown and unreasonable sentence," I wanted to mention my stepmother and wrote:

> God has proven that he is not mean by dying our death, by entering into human travail and allowing us to see his weakness, his vulnerability, his love. . . .

Eventually I moved towards resolving suffering and moral conflict with Paul's own resolution, "thanks be," and termed his faith not absurd but "all that's left . . . the last word."

My father did not die when I was in California, and yet I prayed that he would, or I should say, that he would for his own sake, at any time; but he did about three days later. I had taken care of all the details of the burial with my stepmother ahead of time, and my son attended the burial. When at home again, I typed a quick copy on Saturday after writing three drafts in California. I did not have an opportunity for my secretary to type it for me, so I finished the final draft on Saturday night.

Documentation of Sources
a. The Epistle to the Romans 7:14–20
b. Anders Nygren, *Commentary on Romans*
c. *Interpreter's Bible,* Volume 9

Number of Drafts and Time Taken
Four drafts, fifteen hours

Last Minute Changes of Thought
My last minute thoughts were to place my father and my own conversion into context so that suffering could be understood by faith (in this case Paul's faith), even though seemingly unjust.

Possible Revision of Intention
I did not change the intention of this sermon at its conclusion.

Hearing Group's Response
S.B.   Saw the central theme as the revealing of one's needs to God—of not denying one's humanity. She found

the personalization of that theme in your discussion of your experience with your father overwhelming and she responded to the way you used the reading from Paul to tie in with your beginnings—giving us a sense of the continuity in your life. Paul has been important for Susan, too, and she feels he is probably important to most people. Thus, although (maybe *because* that's my comment) the sermon was personalized, it was not particularized.

W.B. Found this the least intellectual of your sermons. This was said as a compliment—what he was responding to, favorably, was that there were not a lot of quotes, but that instead you were speaking in a direct straightforward way from your mind, of course, but also from your heart. He found your discussion of your experience with your father to be relevant to the Paul reading (which he thought you delivered very clearly) but he responded even more to the fact that you felt free enough and comfortable enough at Epiphany to say these things that were obviously important for you to say.

N.P. Found the sermon powerful and moving. He responded to your clear affirmation of faith in light of your recent experience. He sees this as the best kind of evangelism—Christianity as a learning process in which suffering brings us to the final great questions. He responded especially well because he saw the sermon not as a conscious rhetorical achievement, but as a result of finding the depth of meaning in a human event. Unlike Susan and Walter, however, he thought the Paul reading not the right text for this sermon. But the theme of Christianity as involvement he thought very important and the use of your experience with your father as an affirmation was excellent. We all agreed with that last observation, Susan saying that you often share your doubts with us and that it felt very good to have you share this affirmation.

J.K. "I, too, responded to the theme of affirmation especially because (maybe, only because) it was not the sentimental, glossing-over kind of affirmation that we often encounter. It was clearly an affirmation that came from a tough look at and a deep experience of a most difficult situation. That you could share that with your congregation must give you a great feeling—I know it gave this part of your congregation a great feeling—and I suspect the whole congregation was moved."

Sermon Number Three

CONFRONTATION

Confrontation between countries and individuals need not end in bitterness but in health.

While the Gospel for this first Sunday in Advent describes "signs in sun and moon and stars, and upon the earth distress of nations," the text does not indicate that political and moral earthquakes of a cosmic, national, and personal magnitude are without redemption. Jesus was one of the few religious teachers who taught people not to panic in distressing times, nor to take advantage of social upheaval for political, religious, or personal gain. He said when the earth shakes and the sky becomes darkened and the seas roar, that the world is *not* coming to an end. In fact, there is reason to hope during times of disturbing change because we know we do not grow unless we are challenged. This season of Advent is a time to prepare for the *way* Christ comes. He appears in an unexpected fashion, not as a fierce and unbending Ayatollah, but as an innocent and vulnerable baby; not as a vengeful political messiah, but as a forgiving victim of crucifixion; not as a triumphant national and military leader, but as a Savior whose symbol is a dove, not a sword.

The whole country has experienced the meaning of Advent in recent days as we wait the release of American hostages in Iran. We do not know how the confrontation between our two countries will end; whether or not we will maintain national honor, secure the release of the hostages, and deal creatively with the Middle East in the future.

Yet the function of Advent is to prepare us for the unexpected, just as Christianity's function is not only to bring us comfort, but to goad us into new action. If religion's function were only to bring mindless comfort, it would be a denial of life, for as we see each day, and especially now, life does not so serve us. Rather Christianity discloses a way to deal with the peace-disturbing aspects of human existence and transmutes them into good. It was not in vain that the church fathers taught that the soul could only mature through a pilgrimage which includes experiencing bitterness.

Early church father Origen once wrote a treatise in which he compared our individual spiritual journey with that of the wandering Israelites in the desert. As the children of God the Israelites moved from slavery to the promised land and experienced all the privations of a country trying to find a place for itself. Iran is also a country which is trying to find its soul today, but it is in slavery to bitterness. An editorial in the *Times* last week wrote of the Ayatollah:

> The world understands the difference between a saint and a cynic, between an ascetic man of holiness and a primitive man of hate.

How much is a whole nation like one human being! How deep are the wells of bitterness in us all, how like bottomless pits, black holes, universes of darkness! Origen described the people of God as camping by the waters of bitterness, but because they kept moving they escaped the polluting effects and reached their goal. But countries and individuals often refuse to leave these waters because they are imprisoned by a past and are fearful of the unexpected. They drink deeply and they become hardened. Iran now is a cynical country, thirsting for revenge. To be sure they have had their share of wrongs; to be sure, they have been oppressed; to be sure, they have a list of grievances, but so do we all. . . .

Which one of us has not tasted these waters ourselves? But

Origen reminds us that the children of Israel continued their pilgrimage and came to a place of sweet water, then endured the wilderness of sin, and finally arrived at Raphaca, which means "health" in Hebrew. The progress of a single soul towards God is prompted by bitterness and finds health after temptation, but the worst part of this journey is its beginning.

Bitterness is a spiritual mire, a pitfall which prevents us from moving into freedom, from seeing all of life, its pain and its joy, as an advent, a preparation, a forerunner of greater things to come.

Even though all confrontation is trying and difficult, there are often wholesome results. For example, our diplomatic war with Iran reveals some signs of redemption.

When has a powerful country, used to major conflagrations in the context of the cold war, been so patient with a small irrational country?

When has a giant not crushed the mosquito which has drawn blood from its arm?

When has the virtue of remaining calm under pressure become a lesson for less secure countries?

When has a small, disorganized country caused a powerful one to become unified in determination and to appreciate more deeply its own traditions, forms of religious expression, and values?

When has the religion of a false messiah been shown for what it is—a basis for lies, threats, intimidation, and bitterness—while true religion is always merciful and forgiving? God never used fear to bring us to our knees (or to our senses) but only the emancipating example of sacrificial love.

When has the breaking of international law renewed efforts to keep the law so much that there may be a new respect for it by the major nations of the Earth?

When has there been such an international example of the clear-cut difference between the moral persuasion of remaining resolute and the immoral position of a hardened heart?

Pharaoh, Origen wrote, hardened his heart against the Jews and his bitterness initiated their flight from tyranny. And now more than forty-nine hostages are held against their wills by a modern pharaoh who will not let them go! Pharaohs do not need powerful countries to exist, only a climate of bitterness, just like any of us who acts from deep insecurity.

Let us hope that the "signs in the sun and the moon and stars and upon the Earth distress of nations in perplexity" will teach us that the Kingdom of God is nearer than we thought, that we have more moral reserve as a nation than we conceived, and that we do possess the ability to transmute bitterness, in the long run, into health.

Advent prepares us for the *way* Christ comes to us, and, as Luke suggests, his confrontation of love for this world contains the seeds of new hope for all mankind.

Personal Record and Discussion of Sermon

Sources of Inspiration

The first thoughts for this sermon came from my concern for the hostages taken in the assault by terrorists on the American Embassy in Iran, as well as from the consequent anxieties of parishioners and friends concerning the plight of these 51 captive, innocent people. It was Advent, and Christmas was near; how could I address this international situation in a way that would help people to cope with its conflicts? Also, the religious imagery of an unbending Ayatollah contrasted vividly with the figure of Jesus on the Cross. While I understood the sociological causes of the Iranian revolution, the climate of bitterness which seemed to accompany it needed to be analyzed and placed in context. Confrontation between the two countries caused me to think of the text for the first Sunday in Advent, which concerned "signs in sun and moon and stars, and upon the earth distress of nations."

Choice of Method

I chose "pastoral situation" as a source and moved to the text, using "cultural sources," "conflict" as well as "text."

Intention of Sermon

My intention was to speak to the sociological and spiritual elements of the revolution and its impact on the United States for my parishioners.

Personal Record

It was important for me to provide some meaning to my listeners of what had happened. A thoughtful editorial in the *Times* caught my attention early in the week and it helped form the basis for the sermon. "The world understands the difference between a saint and a cynic, between an ascetic man of holiness and a primitive man of hate."

The next day, Wednesday, I visited a nearby Roman Catholic bookstore and picked up, by chance, a book on Origen and thumbed through it. I read a section which was Origen's exegesis of the pilgrimage of the Israelites to the Promised Land and their camping en route by the "waters of bitterness." I read the chapter at home, outlining the spiritual meaning of Origen's interpretation of the Exodus, and then applied it to the people of Iran. "Iran is . . . a country trying to find its soul today," I wrote in my first draft at night after dinner in my apartment. "But it is in slavery to bitterness." Then a little "spark" was ignited in my imagination. Iran was not moving on past "bitterness," it had drunk too deeply of the polluting effects of that poisoned well and was "imprisoned by the past." I tried to compare their just grievances to our own; "which one of us has not tasted these waters ourselves," I asked.

I began typing a second draft on Thursday, thinking of how bitterness prevents us from seeing all of life, its pain and its joy, as an "advent . . . of greater things to come." The season of Advent is preparation and has a ring of anticipation.

Finally I thought of Pharaoh, who would not let his people go. "Pharaohs do not need powerful countries to exist, only a climate of bitterness."

When I approached my last draft, and before I handed it to my secretary to be typed, I included our need for "moral reserve" as a nation to withstand the crisis.

Documentation of Sources
a. *The New York Times,* November 29, 1979
b. St. Luke 21:25
c. Origen, *The Classics of Western Spirituality*
d. *The Interpreter's Bible,* Volume 7

Number of Drafts and Time Taken
Three drafts, twelve hours

Last Minute Changes of Thought
There were no major changes, only a rewording of the prose for better listening. I emphasized that our whole country had experienced a kind of "advent" in recent days.

Possible Revision of Intention
I stayed with my purpose to address the pastoral situation of bitterness in the Iranian revolution.

6

The Conflict Method

The fourth method of preparing a sermon includes frustration, anger, and doubt. It also allows our struggle to write a sermon, or our effort to be properly appreciative of a text in Holy Scripture, to show in our sermon. There are times when a text which faces us on the coming Sunday is at odds with our own faith, or at least with our own personal understanding of the Faith. Sometimes I am deeply antagonized by a text or personally and spiritually upset by it, and my own negative response to it produces the sermon. For example, I am still worrying about Jesus' words, "Consider the lilies in the fields; they do not work, they do not spin." I see lilies only in New York City when they are grown in the country and cut for our altar vases.

Everyone in the city is in a frenzy to work, at least those who have job-mobility and high expectations; and all of us "spin" our wheels, so to speak. Even the poverty level income people of this city are anxious, and their anxiety (which Jesus tells us not to have) breeds drug addiction, alcoholism, and petty or violent crime. I am not above all the influences from the environment, nor am I able to retreat into an idealistic, ivy-covered city church, although my church outwardly looks this way in the summer. I cannot pretend that the gathered Christian community alone is the only source of urban inspiration. Indeed I have a watchful eye on my neighbors, how they live, what they wear (again I am at odds with Matthew), how they look, where they seem to be going in life.

Another statement from Matthew gives me difficulty: "Do not give dogs what is holy; do not throw your pearls to pigs." If no one is good but God alone, then who are the dogs? I, too, take God's "pearls" for granted, and how do I know if my soul's health has been deprived because I am classified as one of those unappreciative dogs! Archbishop of Canterbury Robert Runcie grows pigs, not for a living, but for fun, and I suppose he has never thrown them any pearls, in keeping with Scripture. The fundamentalists would certainly be happy with him for this, but otherwise there are texts which are difficult to reconcile without conflict, or without using some means of resolving conflict.

That is why I suggest a dialectical approach; first, a thesis; then an antithesis; and, finally, some synthesis to assist in writing a sermon on an obstinate text. I have said before that my own love/hate relationship with Scripture, or with some "brokenness of life," can produce a sermon, and that this method should be considered as valid as any other. In a way it is a method which is an inversion of the first method discussed, the text method.

The text method assumes that Scripture has caused one to be inspired almost directly without great conflict, without saying to oneself, "I cannot, I will not preach on this text." Rather, I encourage preaching on a difficult text, allowing the conflict to show. Chances are the congregation has more doubt than you do about the efficacy of some passages of Holy Writ, and will appreciate an honest sharing of such a conflict. This method is the shadow, perhaps the alter ego, of the first. One does begin with the text, but then in the latter a reaction occurs against the text personally. Such frustration can influence us to find "cultural sources" (like Albert Camus and his works) to support one's own negative feelings in order to speak to the human and pastoral situation. This is not to say that one announces his dislike for the text from the pulpit; but rather sharing the struggle to write a sermon from a text which seems personally obscure means that one is being faithful, that *you* are doing your best to help even a text you cannot accept come alive. This is like the discipline of prayer on days when we do not feel like praying.

The theology behind this method is, of course, related to "conflict." We live in a less than perfect world. The Kingdom of God has not yet come. Tragedy seems often more descriptive of life than transformation of tragedy through the Cross and the Resurrection of Jesus Christ. We live in a post-Holocaust world, in which one half of the world is aiming its nuclear warheads at the other, in which an attempted assassination against the President of the United States of America happens one day, while on another the Pope is shot when blessing pilgrims in Vatican Square. I am a sinful man—in spite of Reinhold Niebuhr's hope that one man can be ethical, even though ethics breaks down in society. There is always brokenness in life, and that brokenness wells up within us frequently as we confront or are confronted by the text for the coming Sunday. Any tension which results from the "ideal" of Scripture (as it may seem on any given occasion to the preacher) and the "real" nature of the world, which tends to crucify or be crucified itself from its own misuse of power, can cause us to begin writing. Conflict initiates creativity; it can be a great source for a sermon.

When I argue with the implications of the text, "Be not anxious," for example, and know myself to be a "worrier," that if I did not worry I would show a lack of concern for others, I also discover that conflict has already started me to think about what I am to write and say. In fact, if I were not anxious I could not produce a sermon—it is the conflict and the creativity in the study, the struggle to write a sermon, which this book basically concerns. Therefore, I have given this method a theological underpinning of "tension" between opposites or extremes, as I challenge the text or share temporal experience, as I reveal my anxiety about its application to the present and to the needs of people.

Sermon Number One

PARTICIPATION

When Jesus saw their faith, he said to the paralyzed man, "My son, your sins are forgiven."—Mark 2

People who have learned to work together discover that their shared efforts often free paralyzed people and liberate paralyzed situations. Jesus did not respond with forgiveness because of the sick man's faith but because of the faith of this man's friends, who together were able to surmount obstacles in order to solve a problem. One of the most difficult things to learn is that God works not only through each of us alone but also through all of us together, the body of Christ. As Ben Franklin's familiar words put it: "We either hang together, or we hang separately."

Confession, it is claimed, is good for the soul, and so today I offer a kind of confession concerning forgiveness and confidence, with apologies to St. Augustine. The concept of forgiveness, let alone its personal meaning in our lives, is often more difficult to accept than the reality of our sins. Years of guilt weigh heavily on our soul and have a depressing effect on our spirit, even though that guilt may not always be conscious. To be sure, much of guilt has to do with decisions which cannot be reversed and which have changed us—from major political conflict situations like Iran to such an everyday mistake as turning down a wrong street which leads to a fatal accident. I believe that too many of us, however, act as if we are guilty until proven innocent, and for whatever personal reasons—especially clergy, we work hard at proving our own innocence when we really have serious doubts about it. Some of our guilt is of course perfectly normal. After all, there is a great gulf between my history and my deeds and the history of the mighty acts of God, and I should have a proper respect for the mystery of ultimate holiness. But, on the other hand, there is the temptation for each of us to try to surmount the great divide between reality and expectation by ourselves alone, as if others weren't also called to serve. We forget that in this story no human alone could have saved the paralyzed man, only a team of helpers who had enough confidence in Christ to bring an invalid to the great healer in the most practical way possible.

Consequently, when we do not feel able to participate we often cry, "Lord, I am not worthy," and when we feel worthless we lose confidence. The world thus becomes an unfair, unequitable, and unhappy place. Perhaps somewhere in the darker regions of our psyche are recollections of occasions when we seemed to be of little use to someone who loved and needed us, to some situation which seemed to be out of our control, to some unfortunate poor sick person we could not help. Ambivalence concerning our own worth as well as the ultimate goodness of the world can lead to self-doubt.

However, without a measure of doubt we would not take that second look at some immediate conflict situation we face, and the few minutes we pause to meditate may place sufficient distance between ourselves and that which worries us so that we become more effective. Yet in the long run doubt does not resolve conflict, only confidence does. When I have been called upon to manage conflict as a pastor, I have made mistakes mainly because I could not objectify that which worried me personally.

On the other hand, when I seemed to have helped people or groups it has been when I have felt confident enough to reach out to others for help, and this kind of confidence is in a unique way linked to forgiveness. If we can't forgive our own failings, then how can we accept others in this imperfect world, and if we can't accept people for what they are, we can't help them. The great absolution by Christ on the cross, his atoning death for the sins of us all, is more than an abstract theological declaration that our private list of peccadillos is forgotten. A Roman Catholic priest once said that hearing the confessions of some serious innocent nuns several years ago was like "being stoned to death with popcorn."

Forgiveness of sins really embraces our total selves: it is living with the ultimate confidence that I don't have to be right all the time to prove myself; that I can identify that guilt which is driving me and find a more positive motivation; that I can accept that good and bad in me which has come through my genes, my birth and my birthplace, my family or my lack of it, my education or my lack of it, my decision-making for better or for worse. Forgiveness is realizing that God does not accept me because I am good but because he is good! Therefore all the situations in which I have sinned (and I speak here of the more important sins which are those of the heart instead of the flesh) and which are identified with pride, that is, controlling, pushing, demanding, and expecting, can be seen for what they are. While I am called to be responsible, I am also quite expendable. Every priest knows that the church he or she serves will long outlast him/her, and the best of political leaders realize this truth of the world as well. Dag Hammarskjold once wisely wrote:

> You will know life and be acknowledged by it according to your degree of transparency, your capacity, that is, to vanish as an end, and remain purely as a means.

In the Gospel today it is the faith of four people who have gone to the trouble of lowering a sick man through a rooftop which causes Jesus to respond. It is not even the faith of the man who is ill which prompts him to forgive sin—which in those days was assumed to be the cause for sickness. Jesus knew that these people went out of their way for someone who could have been easily forgotten and cast aside. Therefore, to the irritation of the scribes and pharisees who held the common belief of the day that sin was associated with sickness, he pronounced an absolute absolution, and the man was released from his bondage.

Through the faith of others we also find release from paralyzing guilt. We discover a confidence which comes from helping them, and we can say, "All this does not depend upon me alone because I have learned to share the burdens I carry with others." The text elicits from us this confession: "I cannot carry this sick man alone." It takes all of us participating together to help those who truly need us, whether a person or a project supported by Venture in Mission or the immediate plight of people in our local community. And our personal healing comes as we are emancipated from carrying a burden imagined to be ours alone. There is nothing more ultimate for a Christian than forgiveness. We work for the goals of mutual service, which are beyond those inspired by pride alone, in order that more and more paralyzed persons may be freed by a forgiving God.

You are the means to that end. Without you, the church is lost: with each of you, we can claim the confidence which results from working together as the Body of Christ.

Personal Record and Discussion of Sermon

Sources of Inspiration
The inspiration of this sermon came from my personal challenge of the text, "When Jesus saw their faith, he said to the paralyzed man, 'My son, your sins are forgiven.' " Forgiveness of sins is often more difficult to accept than our guilt, and guilt can be paralyzing. I have wrestled with "forgiveness of sins" all my life, and this conflict led me into the church. Even after ordination I have wished many times to experience its release and to share the joy of forgiveness with others. Many of us feel bound by the past; it is freedom from this bondage which many seek, and so I have preached the Good News as I have known about it, but not always as I have experienced it.

Choice of Method
The choice of method was "conflict" and I attempted to be somewhat dialectical: that is, thesis: forgiveness; antithesis: guilt; synthesis: "through the faith of others we also find release from paralyzing guilt." Then I moved to text, found sources to help my points, and spoke to the pastoral situation.

Intention of Sermon

My intention was to offer some soul-searching way to conclude that forgiveness is our release, without overlooking guilt and the necessity to deal with it directly in my sermon.

Personal Record

I began more negatively, I believe, than I concluded. It was my own guilt which led me to cite Augustine and to confess:

> Years of guilt weigh heavily on our soul and have a depressing effect on our spirit, even though that guilt may not always be conscious. To be sure, much of our guilt has to do with decisions which cannot be reversed. . . . I believe that too many of us act, however, as if we are guilty until proven innocent . . . especially clergy.

Then I studied the text more closely and hit upon the idea that "We forget that in this story no human alone could have saved the paralyzed man, only a team of helpers who had enough confidence in Christ to bring an invalid to the great healer in the most practical way possible." Then I mentioned "managing conflict as a pastor through reaching out to others," all part of my confession. Also I remembered a story about a Roman priest describing some auricular confessions as "being stoned to death with popcorn," which provided an opportunity for comic relief from breast-beating.

Finally, I moved to a more positive position by saying, "Forgiveness of sins . . . is living with the ultimate confidence that I don't have to be right all the time to prove myself . . . forgiveness is realizing that God does not accept me because I am good but because he is good!"

My first draft was late in the week and I was rushed, not putting my thoughts down until Thursday, and then typing two drafts in one day. I took my sermon home with me, as I usually do, and worked on it Thursday night so that my secretary could have it later the next day.

Documentation of Sources

a. The Gospel of St. Mark 2:1–12
b. A. E. Harvey, *The Companion to the New Testament*

c. Robert Barnes, *Creative Brooding*, p. 14
d. Dag Hammarskjold, *Markings*, p. 103

Number of Drafts and Time Taken
Three drafts, twelve hours

Last Minute Changes of Thought
My last minute changes were much more positive; indeed I compared the faith of those who helped the invalid to that of the Body of Christ; and the whole idea of participation, or working together, emerged later. I quoted Ben Franklin and Dag Hammarskjold, and worked in my views of leadership. Finally I set the point of the sermon because "we work for goals of mutual service . . . in order that more and more paralyzed persons may be freed by a forgiving God."

Possible Revision of Intention
I realized that I did change my purpose in this sermon. I started out with a conflict reaction to the text which led to a dialectic between forgiveness and guilt. While this beginning formed some of the substance of the sermon, I wound up placing the main thrust in the context of participation. The first lines of the sermon then became: "People who have learned to work together discover that their shared efforts often free paralyzed people and liberate paralyzed situations."

Hearing Group's Response
S.B.   "This was the best sermon yet! It had great emotional impact—in part, as with the last sermon evaluated, because of the sense that you were speaking from your own conviction."

J.N.   "I said of the last sermon that I found it comforting. This time I seemed to hear that being comforted is not enough—that we must get out and help—that what we do outside is important. I find it very appealing to hear Ernie speaking as a vulnerable human being."

W.B.   Responded to the message that we are not alone—that if we accept ourselves we can then reach out to others (but unlike some others in the group, found the mention of VIM an intrusion). He liked the way you dealt with the problem of self-doubt and the need to turn to others.

N.P.   Liked your talking about being human and about how grace works through a corporate structure—bringing a new power into life—that confidence comes from God. However, he felt that it was not quite so clear and focused on a single idea as he would have liked. He felt, almost, that you were aiming at more than one target. Although, as always, he found the sermon well-grounded theologically.

W.B.   Was puzzled about the relevance of the stress on the faith of the friends of the paralytic, but it finally became clear.

S.B.   Reacted especially to the discussion of guilt—said she could sense the relief not only in herself, but in those around her when you stressed that we are forgiven not because *we* are good but because *God* is good.

J.N.   "Like Susan, I felt this sermon had a great emotional impact. At first I was almost overwhelmed with important ideas that I wanted more space to think about—(paralysis and freedom from paralysis, guilt and innocence, faith, etc.)—I felt I wanted to read the sermon instead of hearing it so I could go at my own pace. But then I let go of that desire to control my reactions and let myself be swept along by the flow of images and ideas and found it a very moving experience."

Sermon Number Two

WILDERNESS OF THE CITY

Thereupon the Spirit sent him away into the wilderness.—Mark 1
The Spirit does not send us into the wilderness to escape the

problems of the city. The spirit of God leads us into a struggle with the city, just as Jesus was led into the desert to wrestle with evil.

Do not think that his wilderness experience was a flight from reality. We have romanticized nature as well as politics and economics too much in our age. Henry David Thoreau once wrote, as he turned his back on city life:

> In a pleasant Spring morning all men's sins are forgiven. Through our own recovered innocence we discern the universe.

The belief that nature redeems us and that cities of people corrupt us denies the essence of the wilderness experience of Jesus. As refreshing as it is to travel to the "country" back and forth, to place such a necessary distance between ourselves and the difficulties of urban living has nothing to do with Jesus' time of trial. He did not begin his ministry by going on a retreat in some pleasant Franciscan setting. He did not call the dry desert his brother nor the hot sun his sister. He began his ministry with an intense and lonely spiritual struggle concerning power and powerlessness, which would lead him in due time to the city, to Jerusalem.

All ministries of value begin this way. We fight here against powers which would turn this city into an urban desert. Parts of it in the past have not been called a jungle in vain. Remember it was in the Holy City and not in Galilee, nor by the River Jordan, nor in the desert itself, that Jesus was crucified.

The battle for human worth is being fought in this area today, not some wildlife reserve or Western flatland or mountain. The real battleground of the Spirit is where masses of people congregate, where power is concentrated, and where injustice, poverty, and lack of compassion are most evident.

The struggle is here, it is now, and it is ours, this Lent. In another account of the wilderness experience by St. Matthew, Jesus is offered by Satan the power to turn stones into bread, to overcome human finitude, and to control others without their consent. It is therefore possible to surmise that the power offered to him could be used to establish a Utopia or paradise on earth, but Jesus chose a Kingdom instead in which people through free will, shared leadership, and love of God and neighbor would influence the world for good. Consequently, his choice would never be considered "power," as power is normally conceived by most persons today—superiority, ego superiority, financial superiority, technological superiority, but powerlessness. Later, the powerlessness of the cross, his own infamous sacrifice as the example of persuasive love, would inspire millions to serve others.

Reinhold Niebuhr described the cross as "Christian Realism." In contrast to Thoreau, Niebuhr's Detroit experience as a pastor caused him to write:

> The cross is central to the Christian Religion. . . . The price of all creativity and redemption is pain. . . . Creation is a painful process in which the old does not give way to the new without trying to overcome it.

Part of our struggle in the world today is against naive views about nature as well as about politics and economics. For example, Vietnam may be an aggressor in Cambodia and China may be an aggressor in Vietnam, and I pray Russia will not be an aggressor in China; but most of the world has been appalled by the cruelty of the former Cambodian government. A romantic view of nature combined with disregard for the individual to achieve collective goals—all the heritage of Marxist ideology—may have motivated that government to shift populations from cities to the country. When cities are considered Babylons of evil and only rural communes contain enough purity for a new social system, then we see how millions of people can be murdered for the sake of wrong ideals.

In contrast, our challenge in this city is to affirm individuals and to help them as best we can where they live. In this age of cataclysmic revolutions and violent reactions for and against industrialization, religious leaders like Pope Paul II have urged the whole church to assert the dignity of the individual in each country. To be sure, it is easier to be considered a person with identity in a small town. Perhaps this is why New York City is broken down into manageable neighborhoods. Even Jesus was remembered in his home village when he returned from the desert, although his family rejected his new authority. But in the city we are not so well known unless we join a community, such as this church where we are appreciated not only because we have the support of friends but also because of a theology which proclaims "you are not solely the product of society, you are a special child of God." This is why I believe the church can help people when some social agencies fail, and why you will be hearing more from us about the ways we can help others through Venture in Mission in Lent.

It was in Jerusalem, not the wilderness, that Jesus had his greatest confrontation with evil. Even Satan, who fought for his soul like Mephistopheles did Faust's, took him to the Holy City and challenged him there to assume powers which would deny his Messiahship.

New York, this Lent, is the arena of our struggle, the place of our testing, our trial. I do not have an idealistic outlook about this city, but neither am I fatalistic. I accept the fact that here I have been called, and here I am to serve. The prayer on our leaflet cover stirs me:

> Christ, look upon us in this city
> and keep our sympathy and our pity
> fresh, and our faces heavenward,
> lest we grow hard.

I discovered it at the House of the Redeemer, a retreat center in the city, when the vestry made some important decisions about the immediate future of this parish. It is easy to grow hard here, while dreaming of the innocence of the country.

It would have been a temptation for Jesus to have grown hard as he turned his face to Jerusalem, but he did not . . . because his way had always been to show compassion which healed lepers and raised Lazarus, while keeping his face Heavenward. Perhaps it was his continued focus on the Kingdom which spared him the cynicism which tempts us when we have tried to help others with mixed results. As Christians in the city we live in a tension between the Kingdom of God and the kingdoms of this world, and we bear the tension, like the mark of the cross, on our souls and bodies, and it may be through our brokenness, others will be healed.

While we cannot solve many of our problems we do not despair because we have learned from the Holy City that the cross is the center of meaning in history, not some revolution or retreat from nature.

Therefore, our ministry together is against all things which diminish humanity. At the same time, we resist leaving the city to the unscrupulous and exploitive forces which would produce empty buildings and barren pavement when no profit is involved.

The city is our place of testing. Here we have our wilderness experience. If we will keep our vision that man does not live by bread alone, that the cities of the world are called to be the city of God, and that every human being is a child of God, then perhaps angels of generosity and commitment will minister to us when we have endured our trial.

Let us not become Solzhenitsyns who now peacefully live in the country, but Solzhenitsyns who refuse to allow this city to become a Gulag Archipelago. This is our wilderness. The Spirit has sent us into it.

The struggle is here, it is now, it is ours, this Lent.

Personal Record and Discussion of Sermon
Sources of Inspiration

Lent and my concern for urban problems were the twin foci of my inspiration for this sermon. I had an extremely difficult time in the beginning since I had worked on two meditations for Ash Wednesday, and only late Wednesday night through Saturday day remained for me to come up with a message for Sunday. Finally, at 3:00 A.M. I rose from a sleepless bed and "brainstormed" on paper for about an hour, contrasting the text, "thereupon the Spirit sent him away into the wilderness," with my belief as a city rector, that "wilderness" is not just a desert; the city is a vast wilderness and the Spirit can also send us into it to face our temptations or to succumb to them. Unfortunately, I spent another restless night on Thursday (do all clergy begin Lent this way?) and wrote a second draft in the small hours of the morning before going back to sleep. I was beginning to think that I had given up sleep for Lent.

Choice of Method

The method I chose was the "conflict" method, or a direction, through text, cultural sources, to the pastoral situation.

Intention of Sermon

My original intention was to identify wilderness with the city and to help my parishioners understand that Lent is a time in which God could lead us into a struggle with urban problems.

Personal Record

I argued within myself about Lent's meaning in relation to a contrast of city life with country life. As one who has a country house to help face the problems of the city (or to escape from them) I thought I could address the situation with some honesty. After meditating on the text I identified Jesus' temptations in the desert with those we face in urban difficulties, which meant lifting Jesus' struggle out of historical context and applying it to the life of my listeners. I tried to do this with fidelity to scripture and to the method I chose. The opposite of a desert is the city, but I took liberty with "desert" and contrasted city with country, urban with rural life, the realism of concrete with romanticism of flora and fauna. I chose Henry Thoreau's romantic view of nature as a sentimental escape with which I disagreed. He wrote:

> In a pleasant Spring morning all men's sins are forgiven. Through our recovered innocence we discern the universe.

This world view without a theology of crucifixion and resurrection nears pantheism which is an alternative to Christianity. Jesus did not so romanticize desert; did not call it his "brother" or the hot sun his "sister," rather Jesus' desert became Jerusalem in due time. One was a preparation for the other. I used Reinhold Niebuhr's quotation from *Leaves from the Notebook of a Tamed Cynic:*

> The cross is central to the Christian religion . . . the price of all creativity is pain . . . creativity is a painful process in which the old does not give way to the new without trying to overcome it.

As a contrast to Thoreau, I read in the daily newspaper of Cambodia's recent attempt to move city people to rural communes as an example of a disastrous "romanticism." I also thought of Solzhenitsyn, and as much as I admire him, I know that he is a rural Russian at heart who lives on an isolated estate, and has little sympathy for cities in the United States of America (at least he has so written). In the middle of the night I remembered a saying, which was a synthesis of my thoughts, and which turned me away from cynicism to hope. I used it to describe Jesus' view of the Kingdom, which helped him not to be tempted "to grow hard as he turned his face to Jerusalem."

> Christ, look upon us in this city
> and keep our sympathy and pity
> fresh, and our faces heavenward,
> lest we grow hard.

Finally, I typed my own last draft on Saturday, and after "playing with it" again Saturday night, revised it quickly early on Sunday before the 8:00 A.M. service.

Documentation of Sources
a. The Gospel of Mark 1:9–13
b. A. E. Harvey, *Companion of the New English Bible*
c. R. Niebuhr, *Leaves from the Notebook of a Tamed Cynic*, p. 102
d. Inspiration card, House of the Redeemer (Episcopal Order of the Community of St. Mary)
e. *The New York Times*

Number of Drafts and Time Taken
Four and one-half drafts, twenty hours

Last Minute Changes of Thought

My intention remained the same: to compare the city with the desert and contrast it to the "country," and I developed this intention to the end.

Possible Revision of Intention

The result remained the same, only more fully developed. I added the line: "The struggle is here, it is now, it is ours, this Lent" twice in the sermon. First it appeared on the first page, then at the very end. In fact, I refined this sentence late Saturday night and early Sunday morning.

Hearing Group's Response

N.P. Thought it a very good sermon and most appropriate for what we are doing now. He feels increasingly that you are speaking out of your own experience and he likes that. He found it the most immediately intelligible sermon thus far. "I can honestly say that I was moved by the sermon."

J.N. Sensed that you find it hard to live in the city—that you find it a hard cross to bear but that you may idealize the country—which is hard, too—if a farmer doesn't make a profit, he too goes bankrupt.

W.B. Liked the interaction between sermon and the VIM adult forum problem. He sees the city as a crucible and that the people are being tested—your sermon pointed this up—and that in the city is the full range of the human condition; hence, there is no escape. (But he didn't want you to say, "This is our thrust for Lent"—he found that an intrusion; I, too, felt the point was being made very well implicitly.)

J.K. "I responded to the wilderness theme—I know from my thirty years out of the church (which I now recognize as a kind of wilderness experience) that the wilderness can be many things—superficially—and that we don't have to go to the wilderness!"

N.P.   Bothered by the sense (in sermon) that the wilderness is around us all the time. Felt that the point you
were making and one he agrees with is that when one
can't leave the wilderness one *transcends* it.

N.P.   Reinforced Walter's point, then he, and others
began talking, again, how well it interacted with the forum
program and how good that program and the sermon
were.

Sermon Number Three

REJECTION AND RENEWAL

Much of the preparation for Christmas, as well as the emotional pressure on us during its season, is "humbug," but
Christmas is also an occasion for personal rebirth. St. John's
Gospel reveals a Christ who through giving of himself shows
us the way to salvation: this Messiah who comes to us as a baby
is the light of every human being, and yet he is unrecognized
for what he is.

Jesus came to his own home and his own people rejected
him. He was the unacceptable Messiah. He was too lowly of
origin; too poor to save people. His own townspeople did not
think he was great enough to follow. He could do no miracle
in Nazareth. His authenticity was not irresistible in his home
as it was elsewhere. But what his friends and relatives could not
understand was that "He was not authorized to be a Messiah
who saved through strength, but rather one who saved through
weakness." Jesus was given responsibility to proclaim liberty to
those captives who were willing to listen, and to give sight to
those blind ones who were willing to receive it. Freedom of will
paved his special way. Jesus never cultivated a following for its
own sake. Where his vocation as suffering servant was not accepted, *he* was not accepted, but he clings to his calling to the
end, to death on a cross. To die is to abandon one's human
calling; death, William Eisenhower reminds us, is the logical
extension of vulnerable leadership, of being born in a manger,

of his beginning as an innocent infant. "He was in the world, and the world was made through him, yet the world knew him not. He came to his own home, and his own people received him not."

Maxwell Lehman last week in *The New York Times* wrote about "Midtown Messiahs," who in principle he said were no different from affluent television saviors, who sometimes exploit human greed and grief. He queried a few on the streets about why their truth was superior. One said, "God appointed me." Another stated that, "It explains everything here," and he offered him a pamphlet in Arabic. A third, whom he described as a "gentleman who slowly raised his right hand, pointed a bony finger upward, his face taut with solemnity," declared, "to argue with Messiah is not permitted."

These 42nd Street messiahs probably believe in some special destiny, and they would most likely reject each other's calling. But there was no special "superiority" in Jesus of Nazareth, no discernible unique strength, only admitted weakness. If Jesus challenged anyone it was those who thought they were religiously superior to others, like the pharisees. He was a Messiah who absorbed rejection; he knew that it could be transformed into repentance and new life.

"But to all who received him . . . he gave power to become children of God." It's difficult to feel like a new person at Christmas when there are so many ghosts which haunt us, so many memories of the might-have-been, so many remembrances of past sorrow, so many reminders of self-interest, or of relationships which proved more painful than supportive: we seem to be inundated by these emotional spirits, and we can't deal with them all at once. They hang around us like ornaments on a tree, all collected around one single source when through the year they are dispersed at least and we can cope with them, one by one. They crowd us at Christmas, but if we can see them for what they are, make them materialize so we can identify them, we are no longer haunted. Christmas can actually help us to face them.

Consider *A Christmas Carol* by Charles Dickens. Because of his own greed and his reaction to personal grief, Scrooge rejected the spirit and meaning of Christmas. He refused, you remember, to give help to the poor who were gathered in workhouses in the London of his time, or were "on the tread-mill" where men pushed all day long projections of a wide wheel on a horizontal axis. Obligated to pay taxes which helped to maintain these poor houses, Scrooge saw no need to make a Christmas contribution to the individual poor. But at night the ghost of his partner, Marley, comes to him, and warns him that he will be visited by three spirits. The ghost of the past appears and shows him his childhood once again and he sees his dead sister; the ghost of the present comes and he is shown the happy but poor family of Tiny Tim; and the ghost of the future also arrives and he sees the grave of Tiny Tim, whom he would not help, and his own grave, neglected, uncared for, unremem-bered. He asks, "Are these the shadows of the things that will be or are they the shadows of the things that may be, only?" He prays to have his fate reversed. Then he wakes up on Christ-mas morning, sobbing violently with the spirit, and he cries aloud, "The shadows of the things that would have been may be dispelled. They will be, I know they will." Then he con-fesses, "I don't know how long I have been among the spirits. I don't know anything. I'm quite a baby. Never mind. I don't care. I'd rather be a baby."

In a similar fashion all the humbug of Christmas, the buying and selling, the harried family plans, the encounter with par-ents and friends and spouses and children can be overwhelm-ing if we do not see to the heart of it all, like Scrooge. "And the word became flesh and dwelt among us, full of grace and truth. . . ." At the heart of Christmas is the Messiah, who through weakness saves us, whose very vulnerability is the same as ours, who is our Christ because he becomes just like us. He knows rejection. He is part of each of us, just as each of us now is part of him.

Jesus was too poor to be accepted as a Messiah by his own people, far too lowly. Even Scrooge rejected him when he re-fused to give to the poor. It is in giving that we discover Christ-mas' meaning, not just giving for its own sake, but because Christ gives his whole self to us. When we give to others we share a part of ourselves, we allow someone to take a piece of our life and we let them use it for their own. Something always has to die for something else to be born. Yet to share means to become a liberated, repentant, and hopeful Scrooge, who is not literally turned into a baby, but who feels reborn because he could change that part of himself which kept him from sharing Christmas, he could admit weakness.

We all need to wake up and see that we can dispell our ghosts, as we learn from them. They crowd us for a reason. They help us to see that we are only human, and that we need others even if it includes loss or risk of ourselves. If we are willing to listen and if we are willing to receive new sight, we can be changed, and we can say, "We have beheld his glory." Then Christmas has served its purpose once again. All the shadows of our lives are revealed, and yet we are still loved, accepted, and upheld, no matter our failures, by others, and by God.

Personal Record and Discussion of Sermon

Sources of Inspiration

Christmas is a confusing time for most people, and it is especially so for clergy. The pressure to preach in some original way to a group of strangers is difficult. I say "strangers" because some regular church people leave their regular churches at this time for home celebrations and their place is taken by visitors. Families reunite and instead of new joy there is often hostility, "ghosts" of broken relationships, marriages or of tragedies of lost family members. People drink alcohol more, it is said, at Christmas, and become more depressed. All the while we see Santa Clauses on the sidewalks, hear Christmas music in department stores, watch pedestrians buying Christmas trees on the street corners. There is a happiness in the air but is it new joy and a sense of thanksgiving for life, or simply a manufactured climate created by the rush of the economic season? In any case, I have many personal conflicts about Christmas. The source of inspiration for this sermon came from the contrast of the celebration of the birth of a Messiah with the anxious feelings and encounters many of us have during the annual season of an American Christmas.

Choice of Method

The choice of method was "conflict" because of the dialectical nature of Christmas, the supposed joy "of a savior born to us" with the antithetical feelings of personal worry and anxiety.

Intention of Sermon

My intention was to present a Messiah who through weakness helps us. Therefore our "weaknesses" at Christmas, our conflicts and frustrations, are seen in one who was born to be crucified. When we consider seriously his conflict, Christmas can help us to cope with the many "ghosts" which haunt us. We renew our understanding of its essential message.

Personal Record

I always find it difficult to preach at Christmas and Easter. It is as if I have to "outdo" the Lord, and his working is beyond us all. But I also understand that many visitors will be attending services, attracted for various reasons by the ambiance of Christmas. Yet, it is a time for evangelism, for proclaiming the Gospel in such a way that "strangers" respond, not only with their emotions but with their minds. In 1980 Christmas Eve was on a Wednesday and Christmas Day on Thursday, which meant that I had a short time to write my sermon. Of course, I should have started the week before, planning my message in a systematic manner, but late Advent is too much for me; I worry more about sermon preparation, since Christmas often comes in the middle of the week, than I would for a Sunday sermon.

I began this sermon on a Sunday afternoon. The text is the first chapter of the Gospel of St. John, and it always overwhelms me with its theological prose. I had clipped from an article in *The New York Times* by Maxwell Lehman about "Midtown Messiahs," which impressed me. It was humorous and yet it was also sad. The peddling of religion on 42nd Street has less respect than the sale of pornographic materials, and yet I thought his article was true to form. In the midst of the impersonal hustle of crowds in Times Square are heard the feeble voices of street "Messiahs," all claiming some special truth which is too easily dismissed, ignored, laughed at!

At the same time, I read an article in *The Princeton Seminary Bulletin,* which captured my attention. From it I quoted, "He was not authorized to be a Messiah who saved through strength, but rather one who saved through weakness." The Cross was a "logical extension of a vulnerable leadership of being born in a manger," my words. But I moved on. I approached my typewriter and began my peculiar style of free-flow, fast typewriting, almost as if should I think too deeply in the process I would stop "creating." Words flowed freely. Conflict, we are told, produces creativity. I incorporated "text," "cultural sources," and "conflict" to speak about the "pastoral situation" of Christmas, and on Monday I produced four or five pages of loosely organized thoughts on paper. I took these pages home with me that evening and went over my draft. I kept thinking of "emotional spirits" at Christmas. I wrote, "They hang around us like ornaments on a tree," and then I remembered the *Christmas Carol* by Charles Dickens; a copy of which I did not have. Marley's ghost was not unlike our "emotional spirit" at Christmas. I went to bed.

The next day I called bookstores in the neighborhood and found a paperback copy available of the Dickens story. I bought it and then reread the story, incorporating it in my sermon. In fact, I decided to retell the story, adding it to "Midtown Messiahs" and my reading in *The Princeton Seminary Journal.* "Scrooge" never seemed more real to me. He was the personification of all of us who become depressed at Christmas. I asked, "What was the reason he changed into a generous, loving person?" Facing his past helped him to dispel ghosts. "I'd rather be a baby," he finally resolved, and of course I thought of the Christ child. His "humbug," however, is our own, and his ultimate vulnerability is our goal. I placed "Scrooge" into my sermon.

On Wednesday morning I typed another copy, giving it to my secretary for another draft of easy large print reading. In the afternoon I was ready to preach it at midnight.

Documentation of Sources
   a. Maxwell Lehman, "Street Scene," *The New York Times,* December 19, 1980
   b. The Gospel of John 1:1–10
   c. A. E. Harvey, *Companion to the New Testament*
   d. William Eisenhower, "Speeches on Pulpitismo and Its Cultural Despisers," *The Princeton Theological Seminary Bulletin,* p. 61, Volume I, #1, 1980
   e. Charles Dickens, *A Christmas Carol*

Number of Drafts
Three drafts, eleven hours

Last Minute Changes of Thought
Since I tend to rewrite at the last minute, my conclusion became more sophisticated after reading my work over three or four times. I finally came up with an "up-beat" line: "All the shadows of our lives are revealed, and yet we are still loved, accepted, and upheld, no matter our failures, by others, and by God."

Possible Revision of Intention
I did not revise my intention; perhaps refined, but not revised.

7

Findings

In the previous chapters the procedures involved in this investigation were described and in the last four chapters the format for analysis can be read in detail, including my personal record of preparation, a discussion of the sermon, and the verbatim account of the hearers' response to the first eight sermons. However, about halfway through my original work with the set of eight sermons I discovered that new findings were emerging beyond and aside from the answer to the original question of the project: "Does the conflict and creativity of the preacher in preparing a sermon influence the communicative event of the sermon?" An answer to this question did indeed reveal itself as the evidence of the record of each sermon struggle was sifted in comparison to each set of remarks by the listening group.

As will be explained later, the listeners' responses did not seem to indicate that a *direct* link existed between my struggle to prepare and the hearing group's response. However, I did reach some other interesting conclusions about methods and theological emphases which in some ways surprised me.

Before proceeding to these findings, I should say something about the screening process involved in comparing sermon record with sermon response. One preparatory experience was not compared with all the others to see if any pattern emerged from them as I struggled with each method, nor did I compare in detail any one verbal response in one sermon's verbatim to that person's response to another. For that matter, each entire verbatim was not compared to another nor was any separated from the sermon to which a specific hearing response was related. If we could speak of looking at the evidence "vertically" or "horizontally," I chose not to present to the reader all my responses in a row, so to speak, apart from each sermon. A horizontal or lateral approach was taken to each preparation compared to each response. The findings, therefore, are the result of this singular approach, which have already been presented in the chapters of this book.

Related Sermon Discoveries

This project began by using four methods of sermon preparation. I consciously used a single approach, as far as this was possible, when writing each sermon, but as I reflect on all of the test sermons, I realize that certain methods did overlap, and were not truly separate at all. Even though I disciplined myself as best I could, each sermon, interestingly enough, contained a text somewhere in its content, a cultural source—if only as resource—an area of revealed conflict on my part in writing, and a pastoral situation, or where it may indeed "hurt in the pew."

To be sure, one method dominated each time a sermon was begun, but curiously four of the sermons were more alike than another four. Let me explain.

Sermon number one, for example, motivated by "cultural source" and sermon number two, also "cultural source," both had considerable textual exegesis, as "text" sermons one and two, were meant to have. In each of the four, the text was extremely important to the premises of the sermon, even when in cultural source sermon number two the prime source was Hymn 519 in the *1940 Hymnal* of the Episcopal Church. I also relied heavily on the Old Testament text from Chronicles. In the first two text-based sermons, number one and two, a hymn in the first triggered a story about a boy with leukemia, and on Easter, Hans Küng's words about the Resurrection helped me to use that text.

Now another interesting alliance emerged between the "conflict" or tension sermons and those of "pastoral situation," which contained deep conflicts concerning suffering, evil, and forgiveness, although they were addressed to the incidences of loneliness in hospitals in one and the suffering of my father in the other. Indeed, "pastoral situation" sermon number two contained as much "conflict" concerning my conversion as did "conflict" sermons number one and two. Nor did I leave out a pastoral situation when I addressed the need for participation in the church in "conflict" sermon number one or the need for affirming the city in "conflict" sermon number two. Therefore, the *first conclusion is that two alliances were revealed in my original* eight sermons, one between text and cultural source, and another between conflict and pastoral situation.

Secondly, *all four methods appeared in some way in each sermon.* For example, Uganda's "pastoral situation" of chaos was the dominating example in my second text-based Easter sermon, while the eight-year-old boy in my first parish ministry was the illustration in sermon number one, also text-based. The Easter sermon contained the conflict between Resurrection for history or for eternity, and the Palm Sunday sermon used a direct contrast, "hosanna" with "crucify." In fact, I would go so far as to say that without all four ingredients I would not have had a good sermon. Sermon number one, entitled, "Expanded Horizons, not Expanded Egos," included conflict, that is, between self-centeredness and far-seeing faith as well as the pastoral situation of our annual meeting and the needs of the church. Sermon number two, also a "cultural source" sermon, called "Many Messengers," contained the problem of when to be pastoral and when to be prophetic, the age-old preacher's conflict in the ministry. This sermon's "pastoral situation" was "Christian Community" at my church.

Two sermons which were "conflict"-based and two which were

"pastoral situation"-oriented all used the text with some exegesis, and all had some quotations from non-Biblical sources to reinforce the impact of the sermon.

I also discovered that the most difficult sermons for me to preach were text-based sermons for Palm Sunday and Easter in the original eight. One of the problems involved was the timing of both sermons prepared during a busy time of year. This preacher, upon reflection, appeared to be competing with himself; it is difficult, after twenty years, not to repeat oneself in some way. Yet these two may have been most difficult for me because of a too narrow definition of the text method. I assumed that a sermon from a Biblical source should be more "transcendence"-oriented than "immanence"-based, and yet I could not make either come alive without help from outside sources other than Scripture.

I understand better now that "immanence" is also in the Bible and my theological understanding has certainly expanded. If I have tended to be single-track in method in the past I have also probably been as single-minded about typecasting scripture as "transcendent" alone. The two easiest were the "cultural sources" sermons—perhaps because I was using fresh material as a base and not some text exegeted time and time again in years past. The four most soul-searching were both the "conflict" type sermons and the "pastoral situation" sermons; they were not so difficult in terms of creativity because there was plenty of conflict to spur me on, which is the way I am stimulated to write sermons. This is not to say that the plight of my sexton's wife did not emotionally affect me or that the suffering of my father did not cause deep anguish, but rather that the situation to which I wished to speak was clearly defined. To be sure, I may have had problems with numbers of drafts or with not enough time, but these four were the most involving for me personally and therefore not so complicated or so "dry" as they would have been if I had depended solely on a text, for example, to trigger me into action. Basically, *the more conflict the more creativity.* Some of this has to do with my faith, how I became a Christian, and with my natural inclination to be intuitive rather than analytical.

Some Theological Reflection

Since each sermon included in some way all four methods, it became clear to me that each sermon also included evidence of the four theological emphases of transcendence, immanence, transformation, and tension. In other words, in each there was an intersection of ultimate reality with daily life, the conflicts involved, and then an offering of a hope of transformation of life as it might be. All theological perspectives were involved in each sermon, because in each sermon there was a claim of God as ultimate and "other," yet there was also an affirmation that God is with us and in our life. I did not want to overlook human conflicts but to expose them and show others how much all of us hurt together *with* God. I cannot conceive of a pastoral situation which should not be addressed by the church, and therefore I am a son of Barth, and of Niebuhr, even though tragic circumstance and evil may thwart the best intentions. To be simple, I tried to preach the Cross, and, in fact, did so in each sermon.

Karl Barth had little sympathy with modern liberalism as he conceived it in his lifetime, and he stressed a return to the principles of the Reformation. But Barth was influenced by Kierkegaard and Dostoevski, both of whom were certainly not opposed to human reason. If God's sole revelation is in Christ and his one and only means of communication is the Word of God, then cultural achievement, indeed cultural "sources" are of little worth. So while the uniqueness of Christ is asserted, I do not deny that the Spirit of God is at work in the world as well—otherwise how else could I have been inspired to write a sermon from John Gardner or James Russell Lowell?

Just as the major themes of theology are not really separate, so another finding is that they did not appear to be separate entities in any of my sermons. In fact, as all methods showed up in some way so did the theological emphasis behind the method reveal itself. For example, in sermon number one a cultural source was used, "expanded horizons" as a response to Jesus' invitation, "Follow me." A source considered to contain some natural revelation of God's Kingdom, whether known or not known, assisted me through my own sensitivity to speak of God's transcendent claim on us. I could cite other examples, but the point made is that *as methods overlapped so did theology.* As different methods were explored I discovered new dimensions to my own theological thinking and that what unified my theological understanding was my effort to include all four perspectives in each sermon.

Hearing Group's Response

The committee got off to a slow start in sermon number one, mainly because they were not yet a group which had a life of itself by which enough trust could reveal true feelings. They seemed hesitant, and perhaps a little self-conscious of sharing with one another, which is normal. Even so, the remarks helped me judge whether or not that first sermon had much impact. I think the one comment that struck me the deepest was, "He does not believe that you present yourself as a confident preacher, but you should be. He is theologically sound, no quarrel with what he says." While this in itself does not relate to the one question I asked in this project, "Does the conflict and creativity of the struggle in preparing a sermon influence its response," it is included because it is the response of one person who later changed his mind. The comment taught me that I revealed less naturalness than I thought I did. It made me wonder if I had been especially nervous because that sermon was on the Sunday designated as our annual meeting date, or because it was the celebration of the patronal feast of my church. Perhaps both were factors, which made me appear less sure of myself. But the criticism was helpful, nevertheless.

Some conclusions of the hearing group's response are as follows:

• In each response to a sermon there were affirmative comments and expressions which helped me to judge the effectiveness of the sermon, aside from the method.

• There were critical comments which indicated if a point of the sermon was made in depth or seemed superficial, if the sermon appeared to possess a clear focus, or if the sermon evoked personal reflection. One person said in "pastoral situation" sermon number one, "the pictures of Jesus going apart, to be alone to pray, have been important to me. I suppose because it has always been important to be alone to regenerate." I thought this comment was an authentic example of an "articulated" experience of a sermon.

• The hearing group reacted to me as an individual and compared one sermon to another. One member said, "the trumpet is sounding more clearly" in terms of my growing confidence or ability to present my point.

• The hearing response group appreciated it when I spoke from my own experience rather than from others, that is, from the quotations of others. A comment in "conflict" sermon number two by one person was that, "I was personally moved by the sermon." Yet this expression of "being moved" was most evident in "pastoral situation" sermon number two because it concerned my father's suffering which I shared with them. The hearing group admitted they responded to me, to my sincerity, or to my commitment. Conversely, they noticed when I was seemingly not so convinced of my message. For example, in response to "cultural source" sermon number two, someone said that her mind drifted away for a time and she thought that it might be because asking for money was "difficult for me." She was right. The text-based sermons evoked the least personal response from the group. In the Palm Sunday sermon, one person did not have a clear grasp of the basic point, while another did understand that I was dealing with "unrealistic expectations." Yet two persons agreed that they found "no clear, ringing note." In text sermon number two there was again confusion in the minds of the listeners as to my objective and that the sermon missed a "laser-like quality." Both sermons were preached to a full congregation and both sermons were well-planned for Palm Sunday and Easter.

The one sermon which elicited the clearest, deepest, and most moving response in the hearing group was the one which dealt with my father's illness. The committee said they were overwhelmed by it. They appreciated my willingness to share my own experience and my trust in doing so. One could argue that when one struggles in the study with the "pastoral situation" method of presentation, the response is quickened, but my struggle in writing a sermon was in this particular situation less difficult than my struggle to preach from some definite text. My worst struggles in terms of worry about using a method were in the two text sermons, and they produced the least desirable effect. To be sure, it is true that the more conflict the more creativity, but is it in the study—how hard I struggle to be creative, how hard I work—or is it in the conflict which is most creative *within* me? Is it a matter of number of drafts, or time spent, of emotional concern, or my own conflict which surrounded some special life situation which I brought to the struggle in the study? I conclude that while conflict over a life situation and conflict in the preparation of a sermon are both part of the struggle, it is *the conflict I brought to my method which elicited the most creative response.* Indeed, in the case of the suffering of my father which produced the most heightened response, it was the subject, and my willingness to share, and not so much the method per se, which seemed to make it the most effective one.

A final point is that there was no clear consensus, which I could determine, from the responses of this hearing group which claimed the superiority of one method over another. No one method was particularly more provoking of reaction than another. Of course, this group was never told that I had been using different methods all along. They were completely blind to my work in the study, and so they had no way to evaluate a method themselves. If they had known, it would have destroyed the project and they would have been tempted to evaluate methods, but because they did not know how I prepared each sermon and because I kept each sermon the same in style and presentation, their response was a "one-time" response, triggered simply by their listening to the sermon and their discussion of it by themselves after the fact.

Isolating them from any knowledge of what effort went into the sermon freed them to be honest about what they had heard in church. Their reactions to each sermon were consistently different and not based on my method, as far as I can determine. Therefore, it does not seem that varying methods themselves produces more active and creative responses in a listener, although the discipline of preaching different sermons from different methods has increased my flexibility in preaching. My increased self-awareness of methodology helped me to understand what evoked the most provocative response.

Contribution to Ministry

However, the main question I asked in this project—"Does the struggle in the study influence the eventfulness of the communicative fact?"—can be answered in an affirmative manner, with qualification. My personal struggle to begin, research, and write a sermon is one part of preparation, and another is my own personal conflict which I brought to my struggle. If one states that the suffering of my father, for example in pastoral situation sermon number two, influenced the hearing group's response, then the answer is a definite yes. There was certainly a conflict in me when I wrote the sermon at my father's bedside. But if one tries to say that struggling with one form of preparation rather than another influences the result, then the evidence from the hearing group's responses is negative. In fact, there was less "written" struggle to produce a sermon about my father than there was to write my Easter sermon. Pastoral situation sermon number two produced a more articulated and "moving" experiential response, from both the listening group and from the congregation itself (I had three letters of empathy, not sympathy, from individuals who heard the sermon) than I received on Palm Sunday or Easter in the first two text sermons.

I have learned that the way one works at a sermon is not so important as the conflict one brings to the subject of the sermon, although "pastoral situation" is necessary in every sermon. The four methods I used, text, cultural source, pastoral situation, and conflict, I first identified as different approaches. They were all present in each sermon to some degree, as were the four theological planks they were based upon: transcendence, immanence, transformation, and dialectical tension. It was not expected that the four, as methods and as aspects of my theology, were parts of every sermon I preached, but it is clear that they were. They prove either that in my sermons all four are integral parts or that all sermons which produce positive response touch these four aspects, but this unknown possibility can be taken as a challenge by someone else in another book.

I also learned that I was probably not so much a one-method preacher as I first thought, although the only method I was conscious of applying to my sermons was that which seemed an unsystematic style of brainstorming from any source. Sometime in my twenty-two years of preaching (and my personal theological assumptions which are presented to the reader in Chapter 1 tend to bear me out), I have probably used these methods but in an undisciplined, unconscious, and unsystematic manner. By hit or miss, many of my sermons in the past contained the four plans to be a typical "Hunt" sermon. My "box" in preparation was my inability to reflect on what I was doing, and so my effort to break out of this "box," which in reality had four open sides I never recognized, occurred through this project which forced me to analyze my ways of preparation. This project caused me, and it was a struggle all along, to be comprehensive by using a definite method each time, recording the data, and comparing the data to that of some people who were extremely honest with me. It was a difficult challenge to be conscious of a dominant method each time I preached, but as a result I feel much more free now in preparing a sermon than ever before.

Although varying methods on purpose did not heighten my sensitivity to my own internal conflicts, that is, did not bring them out to be shared more with my listeners in a healing way, I did become much more conscious of the importance of sharing my own humanity with others. Now I know that people want to hear more of personal, and less of academic, conclusions about life and its meaning in relation to the Gospel.

Sermon preparation is also easier for me now. When I sit down with pen and paper or at the typewriter on Tuesdays to begin Sunday's sermon, the chore of preparation is less than it was. If the spice of life is variety then variety of method takes some of the exasperation out of preparation, even though not all the worry. Now I can choose a method, four at least, and know that there are four aspects of each of my sermons.

I have also learned how my theology influences my preaching. The very fact that I organized the theological influences of my life to undergird the assumptions from which I approached methods in preaching was an integrating experience. If theology in some way is ultimate thinking about life situations, then my theology was present in every sermon which always concerned life situations. I know that I am a semi-Barthian, who believes God is at work in the world, nonetheless. My aim is to transform a pastoral situation through my own conflicts about them and through the theology which has been learned from experience and from my church. I indeed try to be an effective communicator within the religious tradition of the Anglican Communion. Earlier I wrote that the problem of preaching resulted from the background of the Episcopal Church in which there is great variation on the emphasis of the importance of the pulpit in comparison to the importance of the altar, and that my own conflict in preparation stimulated me to investigate different ways to prepare my Sunday communicative tomes.

Religious tradition, however, by itself need not hinder serious attempts to be effective in preaching, if one works at preaching in a systematic manner; indeed conflict with the tradition itself, in the form of a love/hate relationship, can be a motivating source for better preaching.

The question has changed for me in this project as it developed. To be sure, the question was, "Does the struggle in the study have anything to do with the eventfulness of the communicative fact?"—but I have discovered, at least from the responses of the listening group, that the *struggle in my soul* influences the congregation more than the struggle in the study. It was not just one method—indeed, as I have said, each method became part of a quadrant containing all. Each sermon had all the ingredients, like my grandmother's recipe, but I learned to write the recipe down for my learning's sake, and perhaps for others.

Reading the response of the hearing group should be an education in itself. It would be beneficial for the reader to read the entire sermon in chapters 3 to 6 before approaching my diary of progress and summary, and then to compare the hearing group's discussion to one's own assessment of preparation in relation to the responses. Doing so might stimulate a practicing pastor to investigate other methods which I do not know.

It would also seem that reading this project would be helpful for the struggling preacher in most denominations to understand that methods per se are not so important as his or her own theological and spiritual life as a man or woman of God. If the end justifies the means in preaching, then it is not the means in sermon preparation but the product in relation to the preacher himself. I hope, however, that few preachers will rely on Phillips Brooks' maxim that preaching is truth conveyed through personality, and that they, too, will investigate, and reflect upon, the means to the sermon end. Perhaps they will find a means which I did not, some methodological "magic" which will make the congregation as attentive to each sermon as it was to the one which concerned my father. Moreover, it might be interesting for someone to vary styles of sermons, the actual format of the sermon itself, or the way it is presented, and test the reaction to each by a hearing response group.

In any case, I have learned that it is the conflict in me, and not necessarily the conflict in writing a sermon, which influences people, while also remembering that varying methods as a discipline is a good and healthy habit. But does my project reveal to others that one particular method produces a heightened response in listeners? The answer is no. Does variation in method influence one's own preaching? The answer is yes. Does the way one works at producing a sermon elevate the preacher's awareness of what he is doing? By all means, but it is for his learning, not for a better response from his listeners.

So it is the struggle of the soul, expressed in a methodical way, which causes increased response to preaching. There are perhaps many methods, but one way, and that is the way of internal conflict shared in faith with fellow Christians more freely. The preparatory experience in the study is not so important as the personal experience of one's own life lived in terms of theological reflection. There is no right method. This project has freed me from being a one-method preacher, or at least from seeing myself as such, by revealing that I should have less anxiety about finding a right method at all.

Basically, my theological and behavioral experience as a child of God, converted in college, challenged in seminary, and chastened by more than twenty years of being a pastor, has formed my theologies of method, indeed my four-part theology of preaching. I have discovered gifts within myself which I did not realize were being used to preach; they have been identified, as well as my theology, in such a way that my preaching has improved and my confidence in my own approaches deepened. Perhaps anyone reading this book will be stimulated to analyze his own preaching and thinking in such a way that he is provided some data to determine the theology behind his preaching, his methodology of approach to preaching, and his ability to influence his listening audience. More importantly, the clergyman's ability to be open to the reflections and remarks of his laity in such a project as this one may indeed enhance his ministry in the parish, as it has for me.

Bibliography

Barth, Karl. *Dogmatics in Outline.* London: SCM Press, 1957.

———. *The Word of God and the Word of Man.* New York: Harper, 1957.

Berdyaev, Nicolas. *Freedom and the Spirit.* Glasgow: The University Press, 1954.

Bultmann, Rudolf. *The Presence of Eternity.* New York: Harper, 1957.

Buttrick, George A., editor. *The Interpreter's Bible.* New York: Abingdon Press, 1954. Volumes 3, 7, 8.

———. *England's Earliest Protestants.* New York: Harper and Row, 1966.

———. *Pastoral Care in Historical Perspective.* New York: Harper and Row, 1964.

Clebsch, William. *American Religious Thought.* Chicago: University of Chicago Press, 1977.

Crites, Stephen. "The Narrative Quality of Experience." JAAR, September 1971. Volume 39, No. 3, p. 291.

Crocher, Lester G., editor. *Don Quixote de La Mancha,* Miguel de Cervantes Saavedra. New York: Washington Square Press, 1969.

Darwin, Bernard, editor. *Oxford Dictionary of Quotations.* Oxford: Oxford University Press, 1955.

Davis, Grady. *Design for Preaching.* Philadelphia: Fortress Press, 1977.

Dostoevski, Fyodor. *The Brothers Karamazov.* New York: Random House, 1950.

Eisenhower, William. "Speeches on Pulpitismo and Its Cultural Despisers," *The Princeton Theological Bulletin,* Volume 1, No. 1, 1980.

Fant, Clyde E. *Preaching for Today.* New York: Harper and Row, 1975.

Fuller, R. H. *Luke's Witness to Jesus Christ.* New York: Association Press, 1958.

Gardner, John. "The World Was Not Designed for Our Personal Enjoyment," *The Stanford Observer,* November 1978, p. 5.

Greer, Edwin, editor. *Origen,* "The Classics of Western Spirituality." New York: Paulist Press, 1979.

Hall, Thor. *The Future Shape of Preaching.* Philadelphia: Fortress Press, 1971.

Hammarskjold, Dag. *Markings.* New York: Knopf, 1966.

Harvey, A. E. *Companion to the New Testament.* Oxford: Oxford University Press, 1970.

Hymnal (1940). New York: The Church Pension Fund, 1940.

Hymnal Companion. New York: The Church Pension Fund, 1940.

Ireson, Gordon. *How Shall They Hear?* London: SPCK, 1957.

Johnson, Howard, editor. *Preaching the Christian Year.* New York: Scribner's, 1957.

Kilby, Clyde S., editor. *A Mind Awake: An Anthology of C. S. Lewis.* New York: Harcourt, Brace, 1969.

Küng, Hans. *On Being a Christian.* New York: Harper & Row, 1977.

Luccock, Halford E. *Unfinished Business.* New York: Harper & Row, 1957.

Melville, Herman. *Billy Budd.* New York: Dutton, 1958.

Miller, Alexander. *The Renewal of Man.* New York: Harper, 1950.

Moltmann, Jürgen. *The Crucified God.* New York: Harper & Row, 1974.

Newbigin, Lesslie. *The Good Shepherd.* Madras: The Christian Literature Society, 1977.

———. *The Household of God.* London: SCM, 1953.

———. *The Reunion of the Church.* London: SCM, 1960.

Nichols, Randall. "Conflict and Creativity: The Dynamics of the Communicative Process in Theological Perspective." Princeton, New Jersey, Princeton Theological Seminary, 1970.

Niebuhr, Reinhold. *Leaves from the Notebook of a Tamed Cynic.* New York: Meridian Press, 1957.

Niebuhr, H. Richard. *Christ and Culture.* New York: Harper, 1951.

Niles, D. T. *The Preacher's Task and the Stone of Stumbling.* New York: Harper, 1958.

Nygren, Anders. *Commentary on Romans.* Philadelphia: Muhlenberg Press, 1944.

Raines, Robert. *Creative Brooding.* New York: Macmillan, 1966.

Sherrill, Lewis Joseph. *The Struggle of the Soul.* New York: Macmillan, 1955.

Smith, JoAnn Kelly. *Free Fall.* Valley Forge: Judson Press, 1975.

Standard Book of Common Prayer, New York: Seabury Press, 1977.

Sykes, Stephen W. *The Integrity of Anglicanism.* New York: Seabury Press, 1978.

Toal, M. F., editor. *The Sunday Sermons of the Great Fathers.* Chicago: Henry Regnery, 1964.

Thody, Philip, editor. *Lyrical and Critical Essays,* Albert Camus. New York: Knopf, 1968.

Van Buren, Paul. *Christ in Our Place.* London: Oliver and Boyd, 1957.

———. *The Secular Meaning of the Gospel.* New York: Macmillan, 1963.

Volkman, Arthur D., editor. *Thoreau on Man and Nature.* New York: Peter Pauper Press, 1960.

Wirt, Sherwood, editor. *Living Quotations for Christians.* New York: Harper & Row, 1974.